Preface

The rapid advancements in the fields of Digital Image Processing and Computer Vision have made these areas of study more critical than ever before. As technologies that underpin a wide range of modern applications, from medical imaging to autonomous vehicles, mastering the concepts in these domains is essential for any student pursuing a career in computer science or related fields. The IGNOU MCS-230 course is designed to provide a comprehensive foundation in these subjects, combining theoretical insights with practical skills.

This book, IGNOU MCS-230 Digital Image Processing and Computer Vision: Previous Year Unsolved Papers, is crafted to serve as a vital resource for students preparing for their exams. Recognizing the importance of rigorous practice in mastering complex subjects, this collection brings together a series of previous year's unsolved papers that reflect the depth and breadth of the MCS-230 syllabus. Each unsolved paper in this book has been carefully selected to cover a range of topics, from the fundamentals of image processing to advanced concepts in computer vision. The questions are designed to challenge students, encouraging them to think critically and apply their knowledge to solve real-world problems. By working through these papers, students will gain a deeper understanding of the subject matter, improve their analytical skills, and build the confidence needed to excel in their exams.

We have included these papers in their original unsolved form to provide students with the opportunity to test their understanding independently. This approach not only reinforces learning but also mimics the exam experience, helping students become familiar with the format and expectations of their final assessments. We encourage students to approach these papers methodically, taking the time to understand each question thoroughly before attempting an answer.

In addition to being a valuable tool for exam preparation, this book is also intended to serve as a resource for ongoing learning. The problems presented in these papers are designed to stimulate further inquiry, prompting students to explore topics in greater depth and seek out additional resources to enhance their understanding.

Our goal in creating this book is to support students in their journey towards mastering Digital Image Processing and Computer Vision. We believe that with diligent practice and a strong grasp of the fundamentals, every student can achieve success in this challenging field. We hope that this collection of unsolved papers will be an indispensable aid in your studies, providing you with the practice and preparation necessary to excel in the MCS-230 course and beyond.

Table of Contents

MCS – 230

Master Of Computer Applications (MCA)
Chapter 1: Term-End Examination, December, 2022
MCS-230: Digital Image Processing and Computer Vision

Time: 3 hours
Maximum Marks: 100

Note: Question no. 1 is compulsory. Attempt any three questions from the rest. (Use of scientific calculation is allowed)

1. (a) Differentiate between Analog Image and Digital Image. Also, explain the term Image File Format. Mention some of the frequently used image file formats. 8

(b) How does digital image relate to signals? Give definition of 1-D and 2-D signals and explain how a 2-D image is expressed in terms of 2-D signals. 8

(c) Explain Discrete Fourier Transform (DFT). Your explanation must include the properties of DFT. Construct a DFT matrix of Order 2. 8

(d) Compare Image Enhancement with Image Restoration. Explain the term "Image Degradation" and define the various types of degradations in any image. 8

(e) What is a Discriminant Function? Compare Linear Discriminant function with Quadratic Discriminant function. Give properties and utility of Linear Discriminant function. 8

2. (a) Compare Sampling and Quantization in context of image digitization. Also, state Shannon-Nyquist theorem and discuss its role in sampling process of any image. 7

(b) If the physical size of a medical image is 8 □ 8 inches and the sampling resolution is 5 cycles/mm, then how many pixels per cycle are required to have a better quality image? Will an image of size 256 □ 256 be enough? 5

(c) Explain the term "Contrast Stretching." How does contrast stretching contribute to image enhancement? Also, discuss the fundamental characteristics of image, i.e., contrast, brightness and intensity. 8

3. (a) Explain Haar transform, with suitable example. Compute the discrete Haar transform of a 2 □ 2 matrix, given N = 2. 7

(b) Explain how image enhancement is better in the frequency domain as compared to spatial domain. Differentiate between image smoothening filters and image sharpening filters. 8

(c) Explain RGB model, with suitable diagram. 5

4. (a) Explain Euclidean Distance Classifier. Write the assumptions under which it turns out that optimal Bayesian classifier is equivalent to minimum Euclidean distance classifier. 7

(b) Differentiate between the following clustering methods: 8

(i) Hierarchical and Non-Hierarchical methods
(ii) Agglomerative and Divisive method

(c) Describe the following quantities used to represent any colour: 5

(i) Chromaticity
(ii) Intensity

5. Write short notes on any **five** of the following: 5 X 4=20

(a) Image representation using pixel model
(b) Binary images
(c) Intensity resolution

(d) Butterworth low-pass filter
(e) Salt and Pepper noise
(f) Mean filters

MCS – 230
Master Of Computer Applications (MCA)
Chapter 2: Term-End Examination, June, 2023
MCS-230: Digital Image Processing and Computer Vision

Time: 3 hours
Maximum Marks: 100

Note: Question no. 1 is compulsory. Attempt any three questions from the rest. (Use of scientific calculation is allowed)

1. (a) Explain the term "Image Acquisition." Compare optical image processing, analog image processing and digital image processing. 8

(b) Explain the term "Image transformation". Also, give its importance in context of digital image processing. Write key steps for image transformation from the spatial domain to frequency domain. 8

(c) Explain Discrete Cosine Transform (DCT). Give advantage of DCT over DFT. Compute DCT matrix of order 2. 8

(d) What are smoothening filters? How do they differ from the sharpening filters? Briefly discuss the role of low pass filters and high pass filter in image restoration. 8

(e) Explain Bayes' theorem with suitable example. Also, discuss the role of Bayes' theorem in Bayes' classifier. Give the properties of Bayes' classifier. 8

2. (a) What is image digitization? Explain the role of quantization in the image digitization, with the help of an example. 7

(b) Given, the dimension of an image as 5×8 inches^2 and the frequency of 500 dots per inch exists in each direction. Determine the number of samples required to preserve the information in the image. Also, discuss the term 'Pixelization error.' 5

(c) What do you understand by the term image enhancement? Specify the objectives of image enhancement techniques. Explain the types of image enhancement techniques with a suitable example for each. 8

3. (a) How do wavelets differ from waves? Explain the properties, possessed by a function to be called as wavelet. Compare wavelet transform with the Fourier transform. 8

(b) Explain image degradation model with suitable block diagram. How noise relates to image degradation? Explain any one noise model. 7

(c) Explain HSI colour model with suitable diagram. 5

4. (a) Explain Linear Discrimination Function. How does it relate or differ from piecewise linear discriminant functions? Write properties of Linear Discriminant Analysis (LDA). 7

(b) Explain the following: 8
(i) Partition based clustering

(ii) K-means clustering

(c) Describe the following quantities, used to represent any colour: 5

(i) Hue

(ii) Saturation

5. Write short notes any five of on the following: 4×5=20

(a) Image representation using vector model

(b) True colour images

(c) Spatial resolution

(d) Ideal low pass filter

(e) Gaussian noise

(f) Band Pass filter

MCS – 230
MASTER OF COMPUTER APPLICATIONS (MCA)
Chapter 3: Term-End Examination, December, 2023
MCS-230: Digital Image Processing and Computer Vision

Time: 3 hours
Maximum Marks: 100

Note: Question no. 1 is compulsory. Attempt any three questions from the rest. (Use of scientific calculation is allowed)

1. (a) What is an imaging system? Compare direct imaging system with the indirect imaging system. Also, explain the term 'image digitization'. 8

(b) Compare orthogonal transform and unitary transform. Also, discuss the properties of both the transforms. 8

(c) Explain the term 'Wavelet' with suitable example. Give properties of wavelets. Differentiate between continuous wavelet transform and discrete wavelet transform. 8

(d) Why do we need to transform an image from spatial domain to frequency domain? Discuss the various categories of frequency domain filters. Also, list the filters under each category. 8

(e) Compare unsupervised learning techniques with supervised learning techniques. Explain the different categories of supervised machine learning algorithms. Also draw block diagram for classical taxonomy of clustering methods. 8

2. (a) What is sampling? Explain the role of sampling in image digitization, with suitable example. 7

(b) Given a gray scale image with aspect ratio of 6: 2 and pixel resolution of 480000 pixels. Calculate the following: 5

(i) Dimensions of image
(ii) Size of image

(c) Write expression for forward and inverse orthogonal transform of an $(N \times N)$ image $f(x, y)$. Given orthogonal matrix

$(A) = \frac{1}{\sqrt{2}}\begin{bmatrix} 1 & 1 \\ 1 & -1 \end{bmatrix}$ 1 image matrix $f = \begin{bmatrix} 1 & 3 \\ 5 & 7 \end{bmatrix}$, determine orthogonal transform and its inverse. 8

3. (a) Explain Discrete Fourier Transform (DFT). Discuss the properties of DFT. Compute the 2-D DFD of the 2×2 image

$f(x,y) = \begin{bmatrix} 1 & 1 \\ 1 & 1 \end{bmatrix}$.

8

(b) What do you understand by shifting the centre of the spectrum? Why is it required? Write the steps to carry out filtering in frequency domain. 7

(c) Explain CMY and CMYK colour models. 5

4. (a) Draw a block diagram to show the learning phases of a supervised learning algorithm. Also, write steps to explain the process of applying supervised machine learning to a real world problem. 7

(b) Explain Agglomerative Hierarchical Clustering. Write steps of general agglomerative clustering algorithm. Also discuss single link and complete link type of agglomerative clustering. 8

(c) Describe the following quantities, used to represent any colour: 5

(i) Brightness
(ii) Contrast

5. Write short notes on any five of the following: 4×5=20

(a) Classification of images on the basis of attributes
(b) Pseudo colour images
(c) Pixel resolution
(d) Gaussian low pass filter
(e) Rayleigh noise
(f) Median filters

Chapter 4: Most Asked Questions Part-A

Q1. What is image processing and how is it different from computer vision?
Answer: Image processing involves the manipulation and analysis of images to improve their quality or extract important features, often through techniques like filtering, segmentation, and enhancement. It focuses on transforming images into more useful representations. Computer vision, on the other hand, goes a step further—it aims to replicate human vision by interpreting and understanding the content of images or video streams, enabling machines to make decisions based on visual data. While image processing is typically a pre-processing step, computer vision includes higher-level tasks such as object detection, recognition, and scene understanding.

Q2. Explain the different types of images in digital image processing.
Answer: In digital image processing, images are generally categorized into binary, grayscale, and color images. Binary images consist of only two colors—usually black and white—and are commonly used in document processing. Grayscale images contain shades of gray ranging from black to white, representing intensity values. These are often used in medical and industrial applications. Color images use color models like RGB or HSV and contain more complex data, as each pixel has multiple color components. These are widely used in media, photography, and real-time vision systems.

Q3. What is the role of image segmentation in computer vision?
Answer: Image segmentation is a fundamental process in computer vision that involves dividing an image into multiple segments or regions to simplify its analysis. The goal of segmentation is to identify objects, boundaries, or specific areas of interest within an image. This process makes it easier for algorithms to analyze the image content and extract meaningful information. Segmentation is widely used in various applications such as medical imaging (to detect tumors or organs), autonomous vehicles (to identify roads and obstacles), and facial recognition systems. Techniques like thresholding, edge detection, region growing, and clustering (e.g., k-means) are commonly used for image segmentation. By reducing the complexity of an image and isolating relevant features, segmentation enables more accurate object detection, tracking, and classification in computer vision systems.

Q4. What are the primary differences between grayscale and color images in digital imaging?
Answer: Grayscale images consist of shades of gray and are represented using a single channel, typically ranging from 0 (black) to 255 (white). Each pixel in a grayscale image has only one intensity value, indicating brightness. In contrast, color images use multiple channels, commonly three (Red, Green, and Blue – RGB), to represent a wide spectrum of colors. Each pixel in an RGB image has three intensity values corresponding to the red, green, and blue components. While grayscale images are simpler and require less storage and computation, color images provide more information and are useful in applications requiring color differentiation, such as object recognition, face detection, and scene understanding. The choice between grayscale and color depends on the application requirements and the complexity of the task.

Q5. Explain the process of edge detection in image processing.
Answer: Edge detection is a crucial technique in image processing that aims to identify points in an image where brightness changes sharply. These points typically represent object boundaries or significant changes in surface orientation. The process involves applying filters or operators to highlight edges. Common methods include the Sobel, Prewitt, and Roberts operators, which compute gradients in the image to detect edges. The Canny edge detector is widely used for its effectiveness, involving steps like noise reduction (using Gaussian filter), gradient calculation, non-maximum suppression, and edge tracking by hysteresis. Edge detection is fundamental in computer vision tasks such as object recognition, image segmentation, and motion detection, as it simplifies image analysis by highlighting structural information.

Q6. What are the common formats used to store digital images?

Answer: Digital images can be stored in various formats, each designed for specific purposes, balancing quality, compression, and compatibility. Common formats include JPEG (Joint Photographic Experts Group), which uses lossy compression to reduce file size and is widely used for photographs. PNG (Portable Network Graphics) supports lossless compression and transparency, making it ideal for web graphics. BMP (Bitmap) is an uncompressed format that retains high-quality images but results in large file sizes. TIFF (Tagged Image File Format) is used in professional photography and scanning due to its support for lossless compression and multiple layers. GIF (Graphics Interchange Format) supports simple animations and limited colors (256-color palette). RAW formats store unprocessed image data from digital cameras, providing high-quality inputs for image processing tasks. The choice of format depends on the application's needs for quality, size, and compatibility.

Q7. How does histogram equalization enhance image contrast?

Answer: Histogram equalization is a technique used to improve the contrast of an image by redistributing its intensity values. It works by spreading out the most frequent intensity values in the image, effectively utilizing the full range of pixel values (0 to 255 in 8-bit images). This results in an image with enhanced contrast, making features more visible and distinguishable. The process involves calculating the histogram (frequency distribution) of the image's intensities, computing the cumulative distribution function (CDF), and then mapping the original pixel values to new ones based on the CDF. Histogram equalization is particularly effective for images with low contrast or those that appear too dark or bright. It is commonly used in medical imaging, satellite imagery, and photography to enhance details and visibility.

Q8. Describe the basic steps in the image acquisition process.

Answer: Image acquisition is the initial step in image processing, involving the capture of an image using a sensing device and converting it into a digital format. The basic steps include: (1) Image Sensing: Using sensors like CCD (Charge-Coupled Device) or CMOS (Complementary Metal-Oxide Semiconductor) to capture light from the scene. (2) Signal Conversion: The sensed optical signal is converted into an electrical signal. (3) Digitization: The analog electrical signal is converted into a digital signal using an analog-to-digital converter (ADC), resulting in a matrix of pixels. (4) Preprocessing: Noise reduction, contrast adjustment, or filtering may be applied to enhance the quality of the image. These steps ensure that the digital image is suitable for further processing and analysis in computer vision applications.

Q9. What is the difference between spatial and frequency domain in image processing?

Answer: In image processing, the spatial domain refers to the representation of an image in terms of its pixel values and their locations. Operations in the spatial domain involve direct manipulation of pixel intensities, such as filtering, convolution, and enhancement techniques. In contrast, the frequency domain represents an image as a combination of sine and cosine waves using transformations like the Fourier Transform. Frequency domain techniques analyze the rate of intensity changes and are useful for tasks like image compression, filtering, and watermarking. While spatial domain methods are intuitive and easier to implement, frequency domain methods provide deeper insights into image structure and are effective in tasks requiring global information, such as noise reduction and image restoration.

Q10. How is image noise classified and handled in computer vision?

Answer: Image noise refers to unwanted variations in pixel intensity caused by sensor limitations, transmission errors, or environmental factors. Noise is classified into various types, including Gaussian noise (normal distribution of pixel values), Salt-and-Pepper noise (random black and white pixels), and Speckle noise (multiplicative noise common in radar and ultrasound images). Handling noise involves filtering techniques such as mean, median, and Gaussian filters. Median filters are particularly effective against salt-and-pepper noise, while Gaussian filters are used to smooth images with Gaussian noise. More advanced techniques like bilateral filtering and wavelet-based denoising provide better preservation of image details. Proper noise reduction enhances the quality and reliability of image processing and computer vision tasks, such as object detection and image segmentation.

Q11. What is the difference between digital and analog image processing?
Answer: Digital image processing uses digital computers to manipulate digital images through mathematical operations. It allows for noise removal, image enhancement, and segmentation using algorithms. Analog image processing, on the other hand, deals with two-dimensional analog signals such as photographs and printouts, and involves methods like optical filtering. Digital methods are more flexible, accurate, and widely used due to the availability of computers and digital cameras.

Q12. Explain the concept of image enhancement in the spatial domain.
Answer: Image enhancement in the spatial domain involves direct manipulation of the pixels of an image. Techniques like contrast stretching, histogram equalization, and image sharpening fall into this category. The goal is to improve the visual appearance or highlight certain features of the image by modifying pixel intensity values without altering the underlying data content. Spatial domain methods are straightforward and widely used in medical and satellite imaging.

Q13. What is histogram equalization and how does it enhance images?
Answer: Histogram equalization is a contrast enhancement technique that spreads out the most frequent intensity values in an image. It aims to make the histogram of pixel intensities uniform, which improves the overall contrast. The process adjusts the intensity distribution so that areas of low contrast gain higher visibility, making hidden features in the image more noticeable. It is especially effective in medical imaging and low-light conditions.

Q14. Define the term 'morphological operations' in image processing.
Answer: Morphological operations are a set of image processing techniques that process images based on their shapes. They apply a structuring element to an input image and create an output image of the same size. Basic operations include dilation, erosion, opening, and closing. These operations are primarily used for noise removal, object segmentation, and shape analysis in binary images. They are essential in pre-processing steps in computer vision tasks.

Q15. What is thresholding in image segmentation?
Answer: Thresholding is a simple technique used in image segmentation to separate objects from the background. It converts a grayscale image into a binary image based on a chosen intensity threshold. Pixels with values above the threshold are set to one (white), and those below are set to zero (black). Thresholding is fast and effective for images with high contrast between object and background, commonly used in document image analysis and biometrics.

Q16. What is the difference between global and adaptive thresholding?
Answer: Global thresholding applies a single intensity threshold value across the entire image for segmentation. It works well when the lighting conditions are uniform. Adaptive thresholding, however, calculates the threshold for each pixel based on the pixel intensity of its neighborhood, making it more effective for images with varying illumination. Adaptive methods provide better results in real-world images where shadows or uneven lighting is present.

Q17. Explain the concept of edge detection and its significance.
Answer: Edge detection is the process of identifying significant variations in brightness in an image, which typically indicate object boundaries. It helps in identifying features like lines, curves, and edges that are critical for object recognition and scene understanding. Common methods include Sobel, Prewitt, and Canny edge detectors. Accurate edge detection is vital in applications like face recognition, medical imaging, and autonomous vehicles.

Q18. What are the different types of noise in images?
Answer: Images may be affected by various types of noise such as Gaussian noise, salt-and-pepper noise, speckle noise, and Poisson noise. Gaussian noise is caused by random variations in intensity, common in electronic sensors. Salt-and-pepper noise appears as random black and white pixels and is often due to data transmission errors. Speckle noise is seen in radar and ultrasound images. Each noise type requires a specific filtering technique for effective removal.

Q19. How does the median filter work for noise reduction?
Answer: The median filter is a non-linear filtering technique used to remove salt-and-pepper noise. It works by replacing each pixel's value with the median value of the neighboring pixels within a defined window. Since the median is less sensitive to extreme values, it effectively removes isolated noise points while preserving edge details better than linear filters like mean or Gaussian filters. It is commonly used in digital cameras and fingerprint recognition.

Q20. What is the role of convolution in image processing?
Answer: Convolution is a mathematical operation used to apply filters to images for tasks such as blurring, sharpening, and edge detection. It involves sliding a kernel (filter) across the image and computing the sum of the product of overlapping values. This operation transforms the input image by emphasizing specific features based on the kernel. Convolution is fundamental in both classical image processing and deep learning for feature extraction.

Q21. What is the purpose of using the Gaussian filter in image processing?
Answer: The Gaussian filter is used to smooth images and reduce noise by applying a Gaussian function to the image. It assigns higher weights to pixels near the center of the kernel and lower weights to those further away, thus reducing sharp transitions and blurring the image slightly. This filter is ideal for pre-processing images before applying edge detection or segmentation algorithms, as it helps in minimizing the effects of high-frequency noise.

Q22. Define image restoration and how it differs from image enhancement.
Answer: Image restoration aims to recover an original image that has been degraded by known distortions, such as motion blur or sensor noise, using mathematical models of the degradation and inverse techniques. In contrast, image enhancement focuses on improving the visual quality of an image without necessarily knowing the source of degradation. Restoration seeks accuracy and fidelity to the original scene, while enhancement is more subjective and user-driven.

Q23. What is a Laplacian filter and how is it used in edge detection?
Answer: A Laplacian filter is a second-order derivative operator used to highlight regions of rapid intensity change, thereby identifying edges in an image. It calculates the second derivative of the image, emphasizing areas where intensity changes sharply. Since it is sensitive to noise, it is often combined with a Gaussian filter (Laplacian of Gaussian) to improve accuracy. The Laplacian filter is used in applications like object recognition and image sharpening.

Q24. Explain the concept of image segmentation using clustering techniques.
Answer: Image segmentation through clustering involves grouping pixels with similar features such as color, intensity, or texture. Techniques like K-means clustering assign each pixel to a cluster based on its distance from the cluster center, effectively partitioning the image into regions. This unsupervised approach is useful when prior knowledge of object classes is unavailable and is widely used in medical imaging, satellite image analysis, and facial segmentation.

Q25. What is the use of Principal Component Analysis (PCA) in image processing?
Answer: PCA is a dimensionality reduction technique used in image processing to reduce the number of features while preserving essential information. It transforms correlated pixel values into a set of linearly uncorrelated variables called principal components. PCA is commonly used in face recognition, image compression, and feature extraction. By removing redundant data, it improves computational efficiency and helps in highlighting important structures within an image.

Q26. Describe the basic steps involved in object detection in computer vision.
Answer: Object detection involves identifying and locating objects within an image or video frame. The process includes image pre-processing, feature extraction (using methods like HOG, SIFT, or deep learning), classification (e.g., using SVM or CNNs), and bounding box generation. Modern approaches use models like YOLO or SSD for real-time detection. Applications include surveillance, self-driving cars, and facial recognition systems, where rapid and accurate detection is crucial.

Q27. What is template matching and in which scenarios is it used?
Answer: Template matching is a technique used to find parts of an image that match a template image. It involves sliding the template over the main image and computing a similarity score (e.g., correlation). The best match indicates the presence and location of the template. It is used in quality inspection, object detection, and OCR (Optical Character Recognition), where known patterns need to be identified in varying positions.

Q28. Explain the difference between region growing and region splitting in segmentation.
Answer: Region growing is a pixel-based image segmentation method that starts with seed points and adds neighboring pixels with similar properties until no more pixels satisfy the criteria. Region splitting starts by considering the entire image and recursively divides it into smaller regions until all regions become homogeneous. While region growing is efficient and intuitive, region splitting is better for complex images with varying intensity distributions.

Q29. What is the role of color models in image processing?
Answer: Color models represent the way color information is structured and stored in images. Common models include RGB (Red-Green-Blue), HSV (Hue-Saturation-Value), and YCbCr. These models help in tasks like color correction, segmentation, and object detection. For instance, HSV separates intensity from color, making it useful in object tracking under varying lighting conditions. Choosing the right color model can significantly impact the success of image analysis tasks.

Q30. How is deep learning used in computer vision?
Answer: Deep learning uses neural networks, especially Convolutional Neural Networks (CNNs), to automatically learn features from image data for tasks like classification, detection, and segmentation. Unlike traditional methods that require hand-crafted features, deep learning models learn hierarchical features directly from raw data. Applications include facial recognition, autonomous driving, medical diagnosis, and video surveillance. Its ability to achieve high accuracy with large datasets has revolutionized the field of computer vision.

Q31. What is the importance of the Fourier Transform in image processing?
Answer: The Fourier Transform is essential in image processing for analyzing the frequency components of an image. It converts a spatial domain image into the frequency domain, helping to identify patterns such as edges, textures, and periodic structures. This transformation allows for operations like filtering, compression, and enhancement to be more effectively implemented. High-frequency components highlight abrupt intensity changes (like edges), whereas low-frequency components represent smoother areas. In applications like noise reduction and image restoration, the Fourier Transform plays a pivotal role in isolating and manipulating these frequency characteristics.

Q32. What is edge detection and why is it important in computer vision?
Answer: Edge detection refers to the process of identifying significant transitions in intensity within an image. These transitions usually correspond to object boundaries, texture changes, or other structural information. It is critical in computer vision as it simplifies the image by reducing redundant data while preserving the essential structural properties. Techniques such as the Sobel, Prewitt, and Canny edge detectors are widely used. Edge detection is often the first step in tasks like object recognition, segmentation, and feature extraction, enabling better understanding and analysis of image content.

Q33. Explain the concept of thresholding in image segmentation.
Answer: Thresholding is a simple and widely used method in image segmentation that converts grayscale images into binary images. It works by setting a threshold value, and pixels with intensities above or below this value are categorized into different classes (usually foreground and background). There are global thresholding methods (single threshold for the entire image) and adaptive thresholding methods (threshold changes over regions). This technique is particularly useful in applications like document image analysis, object tracking, and medical imaging, where clear intensity differences exist between regions of interest and the background.

Q34. What are morphological operations and their applications in image processing?
Answer: Morphological operations are non-linear transformations based on the shape or structure of objects in an image, primarily used in binary image processing. The basic operations are dilation and erosion. Dilation adds pixels to object boundaries, while erosion removes pixels from object boundaries. These can be combined into more complex operations like opening (erosion followed by dilation) and closing (dilation followed by erosion). Morphological operations are used for noise removal, shape simplification, hole filling, and boundary extraction, making them essential tools in preprocessing and post-processing stages of image analysis.

Q35. How does histogram equalization enhance image contrast?
Answer: Histogram equalization is a technique used to improve the contrast in images by spreading out the most frequent intensity values. It works by redistributing pixel intensity values to achieve a uniform histogram. This enhances the image's dynamic range and makes details more visible in areas that are overly dark or bright. It's particularly effective for improving the visibility of features in low-contrast images, such as medical images or underexposed photos. Variants like adaptive histogram equalization can be used to better enhance local contrast in different regions of the image.

Q36. What is the role of convolution in image filtering?
Answer: Convolution is a mathematical operation used to apply filters or kernels to images in order to perform tasks like blurring, sharpening, and edge detection. It involves sliding a filter matrix over the image and computing the weighted sum of the neighborhood pixels. The filter determines the type of operation applied; for instance, a Gaussian filter blurs the image, while a Laplacian filter highlights edges. Convolution is fundamental in both traditional image processing and deep learning architectures such as convolutional neural networks (CNNs).

Q37. Describe the concept and benefits of Gaussian blurring.
Answer: Gaussian blurring is a low-pass filtering technique that uses a Gaussian function to smooth images and reduce noise. It reduces image detail by averaging neighboring pixels with a weighted average that decreases with distance from the center. This results in a naturally smooth blur that preserves edges better than other averaging techniques. Gaussian blur is useful in preprocessing steps like noise reduction, image enhancement, and edge detection, and is often used before applying thresholding or edge detection algorithms to reduce false detections.

Q38. What is the difference between RGB and grayscale images?
Answer: RGB images consist of three color channels—Red, Green, and Blue—each representing intensity levels of the respective color. When combined, they form a color image. In contrast, grayscale images have only one channel, representing intensity levels ranging from black (0) to white (255). Grayscale images are used in many image processing applications due to their reduced complexity and data size. While RGB images are essential for tasks involving color analysis, grayscale images are preferred in applications like segmentation, edge detection, and morphological operations.

Q39. Explain the concept of connected components in binary images.
Answer: Connected component analysis identifies and labels distinct groups of connected pixels in binary images. It's based on pixel connectivity—4-connectivity (horizontal and vertical) or 8-connectivity (including diagonals). Each group of connected foreground pixels is assigned a unique label, allowing separate analysis of objects. This is useful in object counting, shape analysis, and region-based segmentation. Connected component labeling is commonly used in document processing (e.g., character segmentation), medical imaging, and computer vision tasks involving object detection.

Q40. What is template matching and how is it used in pattern recognition?
Answer: Template matching is a technique for finding small parts of an image that match a predefined template image. It involves sliding the template across the input image and computing a similarity metric (like cross-correlation or squared differences) at each position. The location with the highest match score is considered the best fit. Template matching is widely used in facial recognition, industrial inspection, character recognition, and motion tracking. Although simple, it can be computationally intensive and sensitive to changes in scale and rotation.

Q51. What is the difference between photogrammetry and computer vision?
Answer: Photogrammetry is the science of making measurements from photographs, typically used in mapping and surveying applications. It focuses on accurate 3D measurements from 2D images. Computer vision, on the other hand, emphasizes enabling machines to interpret and understand visual information similarly to human vision. While photogrammetry is measurement-centric, computer vision encompasses broader tasks like recognition, segmentation, and object detection. The two fields overlap but serve different end goals—precision in measurements versus intelligent interpretation.
Q52. How does image segmentation contribute to object detection?
Answer: Image segment
ation plays a crucial role in object detection by dividing an image into meaningful regions that correspond to different objects or parts of objects. This preprocessing step simplifies the detection task by isolating areas of interest, reducing background noise, and improving accuracy. Techniques such as thresholding, clustering (e.g., k-means), and deep learning (e.g., Mask R-CNN) help identify object boundaries. Accurate segmentation leads to better feature extraction, which ultimately enhances object classification and localization.

Q53. What are the challenges in 3D object recognition in computer vision?
Answer: 3D object recognition presents several challenges including variability in lighting, pose, occlusion, texture, and viewpoint. Complex geometries and background clutter add to the difficulty. Accurate depth data acquisition and the need for high computational resources further complicate the process. Solutions involve 3D shape descriptors, point cloud analysis, deep learning (e.g., 3D CNNs), and multi-view approaches. Despite technological advances, reliable 3D recognition across diverse real-world scenarios remains an open problem.

Q54. Explain the concept of image fusion.
Answer: Image fusion involves combining multiple images of the same scene, often from different sensors or viewpoints, to produce a more informative composite image. It enhances image quality by integrating

complementary information such as spatial details from a high-resolution image and spectral content from a multispectral one. Image fusion techniques include pixel-level (e.g., averaging), feature-level (e.g., wavelet transform), and decision-level methods. Applications range from medical imaging to surveillance and remote sensing.

Q55. What are the basic differences between grayscale and binary images?
Answer: Grayscale images represent intensity values using multiple shades of gray, typically ranging from 0 (black) to 255 (white) in 8-bit images. They contain more detail and are useful in most image processing tasks. Binary images, on the other hand, contain only two pixel values—0 and 1—representing black and white. Binary images are often used in simple shape detection, thresholding, and morphological operations where detailed intensity information is not required.

Q56. Describe the use of computer vision in robotics.
Answer: In robotics, computer vision enables machines to perceive and interact with their environment. It allows robots to detect and recognize objects, navigate spaces, avoid obstacles, and perform tasks like pick-and-place. Techniques such as stereo vision, optical flow, and depth sensing help interpret spatial information. Advanced applications include autonomous vehicles, robotic surgery, and drone navigation. Vision systems are essential for situational awareness and intelligent decision-making in robotics.

Q57. What is the function of a Region of Interest (ROI) in image processing?
Answer: A Region of Interest (ROI) refers to a specific portion of an image selected for analysis or processing. It allows focusing computational resources on relevant areas, improving performance and reducing noise. ROIs are commonly used in tasks like face detection, object tracking, and feature extraction. By isolating the ROI, unnecessary background information is excluded, enabling more accurate and efficient processing.

Q58. What is active contour modeling (snakes) in computer vision?
Answer: Active contour modeling, or "snakes," is a technique used for image segmentation by evolving a curve (contour) to fit the boundaries of an object. The contour is initialized near the target object and then iteratively deforms based on internal forces (smoothness) and external forces (image gradients). Snakes are effective in detecting object edges and shapes, especially when boundaries are not well-defined. They are commonly used in medical imaging and object boundary detection.

Q59. How does color space transformation help in image processing?
Answer: Color space transformation involves converting an image from one color representation to another (e.g., RGB to HSV, YCbCr, or Lab). This transformation can simplify tasks like skin detection, background removal, and color-based segmentation. For instance, in the HSV color space, hue separates color information from brightness, making it easier to detect colors under varying lighting. Different color spaces highlight different aspects of an image, allowing better feature extraction.

Q60. What is the role of feature descriptors in object recognition?
Answer: Feature descriptors capture essential information about image features such as edges, corners, or blobs. They encode patterns in a compact and robust form that can be used to compare features across different images. Popular descriptors include SIFT, SURF, ORB, and HOG. In object recognition, descriptors help in matching objects across scenes or frames, even under scale, rotation, or illumination changes. They form the backbone of many recognition and tracking algorithms.

Q61. What is the significance of the point spread function (PSF) in image processing?
Answer: The point spread function (PSF) describes how a point source of light is represented in an imaging system. It characterizes the response of the system to a single point and indicates the degree of blurring introduced during the image acquisition process. The PSF plays a crucial role in image restoration

techniques, as it helps reverse the distortion or blurring effects. By estimating or measuring the PSF, one can deconvolve an image to enhance its sharpness and clarity. The PSF also assists in evaluating system performance, particularly in optical and medical imaging applications, by analyzing resolution and accuracy.

Q62. How does image thresholding contribute to segmentation?
Answer: Image thresholding is a fundamental technique in image segmentation that separates objects from the background based on pixel intensity. It involves selecting a threshold value, and all pixels with intensity above (or below) this value are classified into a separate region. Thresholding can be global or adaptive, where the threshold changes based on local image properties. This method is widely used due to its simplicity and efficiency, particularly in applications like document image analysis, biomedical imaging, and industrial inspection. Effective thresholding results in binary images that clearly delineate object boundaries, enabling easier object recognition and analysis.

Q63. What is the role of the Radon transform in image analysis?
Answer: The Radon transform is a mathematical technique used to convert spatial domain information into projection data at various angles. It is widely used in computed tomography (CT) and other imaging applications for reconstructing cross-sectional images from projections. The transform integrates image values along lines and provides information about internal structures. In image analysis, it is useful for detecting linear features, enhancing object orientation, and performing shape recognition. Its inversion leads to image reconstruction, making it essential for non-invasive imaging in medical and industrial fields. The Radon transform also aids in identifying rotational and translational symmetries in objects.

Q64. How does image enhancement differ from image restoration?
Answer: Image enhancement and image restoration are both used to improve image quality, but they differ in purpose and approach. Image enhancement focuses on improving visual appearance for human interpretation, often by emphasizing features such as edges or contrast. Techniques include histogram equalization, contrast stretching, and filtering. Image restoration, on the other hand, aims to recover an image that has been degraded by known factors like noise, blur, or distortion. It relies on mathematical models to reverse the degradation process. While enhancement is subjective and application-specific, restoration is more objective and seeks to recreate the original image as closely as possible.

Q65. What is the purpose of histogram equalization in image processing?
Answer: Histogram equalization is a contrast enhancement technique that spreads out the intensity values of an image to utilize the full range of available brightness levels. It enhances the global contrast of an image, especially when the usable data is confined to a narrow range of intensity values. This method improves visibility in underexposed or low-contrast images and is often used in medical imaging, satellite imagery, and photography. The technique works by redistributing the intensity histogram to approximate a uniform distribution, making features more distinguishable. However, it may also introduce artifacts in some cases, especially in images with varying lighting conditions.

Q66. What are moments in image processing and their applications?
Answer: Moments in image processing are statistical measures that capture shape and spatial distribution of pixel intensities. They are used to derive features that describe the size, orientation, and other geometrical properties of objects in an image. There are several types of moments, including raw moments, central moments, and Hu moments. These descriptors are essential in pattern recognition, object tracking, and image classification. For example, Hu moments are invariant to translation, scale, and rotation, making them useful for recognizing shapes regardless of their orientation or size. Moments provide compact and meaningful information for representing complex shapes and regions.

Q67. What is template matching in computer vision?
Answer: Template matching is a technique used to locate a sub-image or template within a larger image by comparing pixel values. It involves sliding the template over the target image and calculating similarity metrics such as correlation, mean squared error, or normalized cross-correlation at each position. The location with the highest similarity score is considered a match. Template matching is commonly used for object detection, pattern recognition, and image alignment tasks. While it is simple and effective for well-defined patterns, it is sensitive to scale, rotation, and lighting changes, and may not perform well with complex or noisy backgrounds.

Q68. What is the function of morphological operations in image processing?
Answer: Morphological operations are techniques based on set theory used for analyzing and processing the structure or shape of objects in binary and grayscale images. The primary operations include dilation, erosion, opening, and closing. Dilation expands object boundaries, while erosion shrinks them. Opening removes small noise, and closing fills small holes. These operations are used in tasks such as noise removal, boundary detection, skeletonization, and object segmentation. Morphological operations are particularly useful in preprocessing steps of computer vision applications like character recognition, medical image analysis, and industrial inspection, where object shape plays a critical role.

Q69. How does object tracking work in video sequences?
Answer: Object tracking involves monitoring the movement of objects across successive frames in a video sequence. It typically begins with object detection, followed by associating detected objects in consecutive frames. Techniques include correlation-based tracking, Kalman filtering, particle filtering, and deep learning-based trackers like Siamese networks. Tracking systems maintain object identity despite challenges like occlusion, lighting variation, and background clutter. Applications include surveillance, autonomous driving, sports analysis, and augmented reality. The effectiveness of tracking depends on reliable feature extraction and robust motion models, ensuring the object remains consistently identifiable throughout the video.

Q70. What is the significance of Fourier transform in image analysis?
Answer: The Fourier transform is a powerful tool in image analysis that decomposes an image into its frequency components. It transforms the spatial domain into the frequency domain, allowing for the analysis of periodic patterns, edges, and textures. The magnitude of the Fourier transform represents the intensity of various frequency components, while the phase contains information about the spatial arrangement. It is widely used in filtering, image compression, and pattern recognition. High-frequency components correspond to edges and noise, while low-frequency components represent smooth regions. By manipulating the frequency spectrum, one can enhance or suppress specific image features.

Q71. Explain the concept of object recognition in computer vision.
Answer: Object recognition in computer vision refers to the process of identifying and locating objects within an image or video. It involves the classification and labeling of objects based on learned patterns. Techniques such as convolutional neural networks (CNNs) are commonly used to extract and compare features. The system is trained on a dataset containing various objects and learns to generalize across different conditions like lighting, orientation, and scale. Object recognition is fundamental in applications like self-driving cars, surveillance systems, and augmented reality, where identifying and interacting with physical entities is crucial for the system's decision-making process.

Q72. What are histograms in image processing, and how are they used?
Answer: Histograms in image processing are graphical representations of the distribution of pixel intensities in a grayscale image. They show the frequency of each intensity level from 0 (black) to 255 (white). Histograms are used for image analysis, enhancement, and thresholding. For example, a low contrast image will have a narrow histogram, and applying histogram equalization can spread the intensity values for better

contrast. Additionally, histograms help in object segmentation, feature extraction, and matching. They are fundamental tools in both pre-processing and decision-making stages of many computer vision applications.

Q73. Describe edge detection and its significance in image processing.
Answer: Edge detection is a technique used to identify significant local changes in intensity in an image. It aims to capture important structural features such as object boundaries and contours. Common edge detection algorithms include the Sobel, Prewitt, Canny, and Laplacian operators. The significance of edge detection lies in its ability to reduce the amount of data in an image while preserving essential geometric information. It forms the basis for higher-level processing like object recognition, segmentation, and image registration. Effective edge detection is critical for accurate and efficient visual understanding.

Q74. How is feature matching performed in computer vision?
Answer: Feature matching in computer vision involves comparing key features (like edges, corners, or blobs) extracted from two or more images to find correspondences. Algorithms such as SIFT (Scale-Invariant Feature Transform), SURF (Speeded-Up Robust Features), and ORB (Oriented FAST and Rotated BRIEF) are commonly used to detect and describe features. The matching is usually performed using distance metrics like Euclidean or Hamming distance. Feature matching is essential for applications like image stitching, 3D reconstruction, motion tracking, and object recognition, where spatial correspondence plays a key role in understanding the scene.

Q75. What are the applications of computer vision in healthcare?
Answer: Computer vision in healthcare has transformative applications, especially in diagnostics, surgery, and patient monitoring. It is used in medical imaging to detect anomalies in X-rays, MRIs, and CT scans through automated analysis. Computer vision aids in tumor detection, fracture identification, and organ segmentation. In surgeries, it supports robotic-assisted procedures by providing real-time visual feedback. Additionally, it facilitates remote patient monitoring through gesture recognition and behavioral analysis. The integration of deep learning models enhances accuracy and reliability, making computer vision a vital component in modern medical technologies.

Q76. Define region-based segmentation and explain its working.
Answer: Region-based segmentation is a method of dividing an image into regions based on predefined criteria such as intensity similarity or texture. It works by grouping neighboring pixels that share similar properties to form meaningful segments. Techniques include region growing, region splitting and merging, and watershed algorithms. The approach starts with a seed pixel and grows the region by including adjacent pixels that satisfy the similarity condition. Region-based methods are useful for extracting specific objects or areas from complex images and are widely used in medical imaging and satellite image analysis.

Q77. What is a convolutional layer in deep learning-based vision systems?
Answer: A convolutional layer is a fundamental building block of convolutional neural networks (CNNs), used extensively in deep learning-based vision systems. It performs convolution operations between the input image and learnable filters (kernels) to extract features like edges, textures, and shapes. Each filter detects specific patterns, and the output is a feature map representing these detected features. The convolutional layer allows for spatial hierarchy learning, enabling the network to recognize complex patterns in deeper layers. This architecture has proven highly effective in image classification, object detection, and face recognition tasks.

Q78. Explain the term 'thresholding' in the context of image processing.
Answer: Thresholding is a technique used in image processing to convert a grayscale image into a binary image. It involves selecting a threshold value and converting all pixels with intensity above the threshold to white (1) and those below it to black (0). Thresholding can be global or adaptive. Global thresholding

applies the same threshold across the entire image, while adaptive thresholding calculates different thresholds for different regions. This method is widely used in document scanning, object detection, and image segmentation where distinguishing foreground from background is essential.

Q79. Describe the use of optical flow in motion analysis.
Answer: Optical flow is a method used to estimate the apparent motion of objects, surfaces, or edges in a visual scene between consecutive frames. It computes a vector field that represents the displacement of pixels over time. Optical flow is crucial for tasks like video stabilization, object tracking, gesture recognition, and autonomous navigation. Algorithms like Lucas-Kanade and Horn-Schunck are commonly used to compute optical flow. By analyzing the flow patterns, systems can infer motion dynamics and predict future positions, enabling intelligent and responsive behavior in computer vision applications.

Q80. What is the significance of Principal Component Analysis (PCA) in image processing?
Answer: Principal Component Analysis (PCA) is a statistical technique used for dimensionality reduction and feature extraction in image processing. It transforms a set of correlated variables into a smaller set of uncorrelated variables called principal components. PCA helps reduce the computational cost and remove redundancy while retaining the most important information. In face recognition, PCA is used to create 'eigenfaces' that represent the variance in facial features. PCA is also employed in image compression, noise reduction, and pattern recognition, making it a valuable tool in both preprocessing and analysis phases.

Q81. How does image smoothing help in computer vision tasks?
Answer: Image smoothing is a preprocessing technique used to reduce noise and minor variations in an image while preserving important structural features. It enhances the quality of the image by applying filters like Gaussian blur, median filter, or bilateral filter. Smoothing is especially helpful before edge detection, object recognition, or segmentation tasks, as it minimizes irrelevant details that can lead to false detections. By averaging out local pixel variations, smoothing helps vision systems focus on the actual shapes and contours, improving the accuracy and reliability of downstream processes.

Q82. What is the difference between morphological dilation and erosion?
Answer: Morphological dilation and erosion are fundamental operations used in binary image processing. Dilation adds pixels to the boundaries of objects, effectively growing or thickening them. This helps in connecting broken parts of an object. Erosion, on the other hand, removes pixels from object boundaries, shrinking them. It is useful for eliminating small noise and separating connected objects. Both operations rely on a structuring element and are often used in sequence (e.g., opening or closing) for tasks like object extraction, noise removal, and shape analysis.

Q83. Explain the role of the Haar cascade classifier in face detection.
Answer: The Haar cascade classifier is an object detection algorithm used for identifying faces and other objects in images or video. It uses a cascade function that is trained with lots of positive and negative images. The features are based on Haar wavelets and computed rapidly using an integral image representation. The classifier consists of multiple stages, each rejecting negative windows and allowing positive ones to pass through. It is computationally efficient and effective in real-time face detection, making it widely used in surveillance, mobile applications, and embedded systems.

Q84. What is image segmentation and its types?
Answer: Image segmentation is the process of partitioning an image into multiple meaningful regions, typically to simplify analysis or locate objects. The main types of image segmentation include threshold-based segmentation, edge-based segmentation, region-based segmentation, and clustering-based methods like k-means. More advanced techniques include semantic segmentation and instance segmentation, often implemented using deep learning models like U-Net or Mask R-CNN. Segmentation is critical in medical

imaging, satellite imagery, and autonomous vehicles, as it helps systems understand and label distinct parts of an image for further analysis.

Q85. What are the advantages of using CNNs in image classification tasks?
Answer: Convolutional Neural Networks (CNNs) offer several advantages in image classification. First, they automatically learn spatial hierarchies of features, which makes them highly efficient in recognizing complex patterns. Second, CNNs require minimal preprocessing compared to traditional methods. Their shared weights and local receptive fields reduce the number of parameters, making them computationally efficient. Additionally, CNNs can handle variations in scale, orientation, and position of objects. These properties make CNNs the backbone of modern image recognition applications such as face detection, handwriting recognition, and scene understanding.

Q86. Describe how a confusion matrix is used in image classification evaluation.
Answer: A confusion matrix is a performance evaluation tool used in classification problems, including image classification. It is a square matrix that compares the predicted labels against the actual labels. Each row represents the instances in a predicted class, while each column represents the instances in an actual class. From this matrix, metrics like accuracy, precision, recall, and F1-score are derived. The confusion matrix helps identify where the model is making errors and which classes are being misclassified, providing valuable insight for model improvement.

Q87. How does the Sobel operator detect edges?
Answer: The Sobel operator detects edges by calculating the gradient of image intensity at each pixel, indicating the direction and strength of the edges. It uses two 3×3 convolution kernels: one for detecting horizontal changes and another for vertical changes. The result of applying these kernels is a pair of gradient components, which are then combined to form the gradient magnitude. The Sobel operator is sensitive to noise but provides better results for thick edges. It is widely used for edge detection in image preprocessing tasks.

Q88. What is active contour (snake) model in segmentation?
Answer: The active contour or snake model is a segmentation technique that detects object boundaries in images. It starts with an initial contour and iteratively evolves it to fit the edges of the object by minimizing an energy function. This energy function combines internal forces (smoothness of the curve) and external forces (image gradients). Snakes are effective in segmenting irregular shapes and are particularly useful in medical imaging and object tracking. The model adapts to object shapes dynamically, making it powerful for applications requiring precision and flexibility.

Q89. Explain the difference between semantic and instance segmentation.
Answer: Semantic segmentation assigns a class label to every pixel in the image, grouping all objects of the same category together. For example, all cars in an image would be labeled as "car." Instance segmentation goes a step further by differentiating between individual objects of the same class, labeling each separately. While semantic segmentation helps in understanding the scene at a pixel level, instance segmentation provides object-level understanding. Instance segmentation is more complex and typically involves models like Mask R-CNN that combine object detection with pixel-level labeling.

Q90. What are corner detection techniques and where are they used?
Answer: Corner detection techniques identify points in an image where the intensity changes significantly in multiple directions, typically at the junction of two edges. Common methods include the Harris Corner Detector and the Shi-Tomasi algorithm. These points are highly distinctive and are used as features in various computer vision tasks like motion tracking, object recognition, and image stitching. Corners provide robust and repeatable keypoints, making them ideal for matching images under different transformations or viewpoints.

Q91. Describe the concept of template matching in image processing.
Answer: Template matching is a technique in image processing used to find a small image (template) within a larger image. It involves sliding the template over the input image and comparing the template and image patches using a similarity measure, such as cross-correlation or sum of squared differences. The location with the highest similarity score is considered a match. Template matching is useful in scenarios where the object appearance is known and does not change much, such as character recognition, quality inspection, and simple object detection.

Q92. What is the use of the Hough Transform in computer vision?
Answer: The Hough Transform is a feature extraction technique used to detect simple geometric shapes like lines, circles, and ellipses in images. It maps points from the image space to a parameter space and identifies accumulations that indicate the presence of a shape. For example, to detect lines, the transform identifies points in the image that lie on the same straight line in Hough space. This method is robust to noise and partial occlusions and is widely used in lane detection in autonomous vehicles and shape recognition.

Q93. Explain the difference between supervised and unsupervised learning in vision systems.
Answer: In supervised learning, the model is trained on a labeled dataset, where each input image has a corresponding output label. It learns to map inputs to outputs and generalizes to unseen data. In unsupervised learning, there are no labels, and the model finds hidden patterns or structures in the data, such as clusters or associations. Supervised learning is used for tasks like image classification and object detection, while unsupervised learning is useful for clustering, anomaly detection, and dimensionality reduction in vision applications.

Q94. What is the difference between 2D and 3D computer vision?
Answer: 2D computer vision deals with flat images and focuses on analyzing pixels and their relationships in a two-dimensional space. Tasks include image classification, edge detection, and segmentation. 3D computer vision, on the other hand, involves understanding depth and spatial relationships, often using multiple images or sensors to reconstruct three-dimensional structures. It is used in applications like 3D modeling, robotics, AR/VR, and object manipulation. While 2D vision offers faster processing, 3D vision provides more accurate spatial understanding of the environment.

Q95. What are feature descriptors in computer vision?
Answer: Feature descriptors are numerical representations that describe the appearance of keypoints or features in an image. They help in comparing and matching features across different images. Common descriptors include SIFT, SURF, ORB, and BRIEF. These descriptors capture local gradients, orientation, and texture information around the feature point. They are crucial in tasks like image stitching, tracking, and object recognition, where matching features across multiple images or frames is necessary for establishing correspondences and making inferences.

Q96. How is background subtraction performed in video analysis?
Answer: Background subtraction is a technique used in video analysis to detect moving objects by separating foreground from a static background. It involves modeling the background scene and comparing each new frame to this model to detect changes. Techniques include frame differencing, running average, Gaussian mixture models (GMM), and deep learning-based approaches. This method is essential in surveillance systems, traffic monitoring, and human-computer interaction, where identifying dynamic elements helps in understanding scene activity.

Q97. What are the challenges in image processing with low-light conditions?
Answer: Low-light conditions present several challenges in image processing, including poor contrast,

increased noise, and color distortion. These issues make it difficult for vision systems to detect features, edges, and objects accurately. Noise reduction, contrast enhancement, and image denoising techniques are essential in such scenarios. Deep learning methods trained on low-light datasets are increasingly being used to enhance images. Handling low-light environments is critical in applications like surveillance, autonomous driving, and night vision systems.

Q98. Explain the role of data augmentation in training vision models.
Answer: Data augmentation is a technique used to artificially expand a training dataset by applying transformations like rotation, scaling, flipping, cropping, and color changes to existing images. It helps improve the generalization of vision models by exposing them to various image distortions and perspectives. This prevents overfitting and improves robustness to real-world scenarios. Data augmentation is especially useful in deep learning where large datasets are required, and it's a standard practice in tasks like classification, detection, and segmentation.

Q99. What is stereo vision and how does it work?
Answer: Stereo vision involves using two or more cameras placed at different viewpoints to capture the same scene. By analyzing the disparity between corresponding points in the images, it estimates depth and creates a 3D representation of the scene. Stereo vision mimics human binocular vision and is used in robotics, autonomous vehicles, and 3D reconstruction. It requires accurate camera calibration and feature matching to compute depth maps, enabling machines to understand spatial relationships and navigate complex environments.

Q100. How do generative adversarial networks (GANs) apply to computer vision?
Answer: Generative Adversarial Networks (GANs) consist of a generator and a discriminator that compete in a zero-sum game. In computer vision, GANs are used for generating realistic images, image super-resolution, image-to-image translation, and style transfer. The generator creates fake images, while the discriminator tries to distinguish real from fake. Over time, the generator learns to produce highly realistic images. GANs have revolutionized synthetic data generation, aiding in training vision models and applications like deepfake creation, art generation, and virtual try-on systems.

Q101. What is the use of Otsu's thresholding in image processing?
Answer: Otsu's thresholding is a global thresholding technique used to automatically perform clustering-based image thresholding. It calculates the optimum threshold separating the image into two classes by minimizing the intra-class variance or maximizing inter-class variance. This method is especially useful for bimodal images where the histogram has two distinct peaks. Otsu's method is efficient and widely used in applications such as document image binarization, medical imaging, and shape analysis.

Q102. What are image pyramids and their applications?
Answer: Image pyramids are a type of multi-scale representation in image processing where an image is repeatedly smoothed and downsampled to create a stack of images with decreasing resolution. There are two types: Gaussian pyramids and Laplacian pyramids. Applications include image blending, object detection at multiple scales, and real-time tracking. Pyramids allow faster processing and better handling of images with features appearing at different scales.

Q103. What is the purpose of the Sobel operator in edge detection?
Answer: The Sobel operator is used to detect edges by calculating the gradient of image intensity at each pixel. It uses convolution kernels to approximate derivatives in the horizontal and vertical directions. The result highlights regions with high spatial frequency, indicating edges. It is especially useful due to its noise-suppressing nature and is often used in applications like computer vision, object tracking, and medical image segmentation.

Q104. How does feature matching work in computer vision?
Answer*:* Feature matching involves finding corresponding points between two or more images. This is done by extracting keypoints (like SIFT, SURF, ORB) and comparing their descriptors using distance metrics (e.g., Euclidean distance). Matched features help in image stitching, 3D reconstruction, and object recognition. Good matches are identified using algorithms like FLANN or brute force, and refined using RANSAC to eliminate outliers.

Q105. Explain the use of Kalman Filter in object tracking.
Answer: The Kalman Filter is a recursive algorithm used to estimate the state of a dynamic system from a series of noisy measurements. In object tracking, it predicts the future position of the object based on its past states and corrects it using current measurements. It is efficient for linear motion models and widely used in applications like autonomous vehicles, gesture recognition, and surveillance systems due to its real-time performance.

Q106. What is the role of the affine transformation in image processing?
Answer: Affine transformation is a linear mapping method that preserves points, straight lines, and planes. It includes operations like rotation, scaling, translation, and shearing. It's used in geometric image transformations such as image alignment, registration, and normalization. Since affine transformations maintain parallelism and ratios of distances, they are particularly useful in applications involving camera calibration and object recognition.

Q107. Describe the concept of the vanishing point in computer vision.
Answer*:* The vanishing point is a point in a perspective image where parallel lines in 3D space appear to converge. It is a key concept in projective geometry and is used in applications such as camera calibration, 3D reconstruction, and scene understanding. By analyzing vanishing points, computer vision systems can infer the orientation of objects and the camera's position relative to the scene.

Q108. How is image sharpening performed?
Answer: Image sharpening is performed to enhance edges and fine details in an image. It typically involves applying a high-pass filter that emphasizes areas of rapid intensity change. Techniques include using Laplacian filters, unsharp masking, and high-boost filtering. Sharpening is useful in applications like satellite imagery, medical diagnostics, and object recognition, but must be carefully controlled to avoid amplifying noise.

Q109. What are the applications of Gabor filters in image processing?
Answer*:* Gabor filters are linear filters used for texture analysis, edge detection, and feature extraction. They are particularly effective in capturing spatial frequency, orientation, and texture properties of an image. Applications include fingerprint recognition, texture segmentation, and face recognition. Gabor filters mimic the response of human visual cortex neurons and are useful in biological and computer vision contexts.

Q110. What is the difference between morphological dilation and erosion?
Answer: Dilation and erosion are basic morphological operations used in binary image processing. Dilation adds pixels to the boundaries of objects, making them grow, while erosion removes pixels on object boundaries, causing them to shrink. These operations are used in noise removal, hole filling, and shape analysis. Combined forms like opening and closing help in object segmentation and feature extraction.

Q111. Explain the importance of Fourier Transform in image processing.
Answer: The Fourier Transform is used to analyze the frequency components of an image. It transforms an image from the spatial domain to the frequency domain. This is useful in filtering, image compression, and

image analysis. It allows for operations like removing periodic noise and enhancing certain frequency components. The inverse Fourier Transform reconstructs the image back to its original form.

Q112. What is the difference between active and passive stereo vision?

Answer: Passive stereo vision uses two or more cameras to capture images from different viewpoints and estimates depth by analyzing disparities between them. Active stereo vision, on the other hand, involves projecting a known pattern (e.g., laser grid) onto the scene to simplify matching and improve accuracy. Active methods work well in low-texture environments, while passive methods rely on natural scene texture.

Q113. Describe the role of image histogram equalization.

Answer: Histogram equalization is a technique for contrast enhancement. It redistributes the intensity values of an image so that they span a wider range, thereby enhancing global contrast. It is particularly effective for improving visibility in images with poor lighting. Applications include medical imaging, satellite imagery, and pre-processing steps for object detection.

Q114. What is disparity in stereo vision and how is it used?

Answer: Disparity refers to the difference in position of the same object in two stereo images taken from slightly different viewpoints. It is inversely proportional to depth and is used to generate disparity maps that help estimate depth in a scene. Disparity is fundamental in 3D reconstruction, autonomous navigation, and robotic vision.

Q115. What is template matching and where is it used?

Answer: Template matching is a technique used to locate instances of a template image within a larger image. It works by sliding the template over the input image and computing a similarity measure (e.g., correlation). It's commonly used in object detection, quality control in manufacturing, and OCR. Though simple, it is computationally expensive and sensitive to scale and rotation.

Q116. How do CNNs work in image classification tasks?

Answer: Convolutional Neural Networks (CNNs) automatically extract hierarchical features from images using convolutional layers, pooling layers, and fully connected layers. They are trained on labeled datasets to learn patterns that differentiate image classes. CNNs are highly effective in tasks like facial recognition, medical image diagnosis, and autonomous driving due to their ability to learn spatial hierarchies of features.

Q117. What is the difference between RGB and HSV color models?

Answer: RGB (Red, Green, Blue) is a color model based on primary colors used in displays, whereas HSV (Hue, Saturation, Value) separates color information (hue) from intensity (value). HSV is more aligned with human perception of color and is often used in image segmentation and color-based tracking. HSV allows easier manipulation of color attributes than RGB.

Q118. What is the Hough Transform and how is it used?

Answer: The Hough Transform is a feature extraction technique used to detect geometric shapes such as lines, circles, and ellipses in images. It works by transforming points in the image space to a parameter space where shapes are detected as peaks. It is widely used in lane detection in autonomous vehicles, shape recognition, and industrial vision systems.

Q119. What are key challenges in real-time image processing?

Answer: Real-time image processing faces challenges such as high computational cost, low latency requirements, limited hardware resources, and noise robustness. Solutions involve algorithm optimization, hardware acceleration (using GPUs), and lightweight models. Applications in surveillance, autonomous driving, and AR/VR require real-time performance without compromising accuracy.

Q120. How does face recognition work using deep learning?
Answer: Deep learning-based face recognition systems use CNNs to learn facial features from images. These models are trained to map faces into an embedding space where similar faces are close together. Techniques like FaceNet and DeepFace utilize triplet loss to enhance accuracy. Applications include biometric authentication, security systems, and social media tagging.

Q121. What is the significance of image stitching in computer vision?
Answer: Image stitching combines multiple overlapping images to create a single panoramic image. It involves keypoint detection, feature matching, homography estimation, and blending. Used in photography, virtual tours, and satellite imaging, stitching enables wide-field visualization and high-resolution imaging of large scenes.

Q122. What is mean shift tracking?
Answer: Mean shift tracking is a non-parametric feature-space analysis technique used for locating the mode of a distribution. It iteratively shifts a kernel window towards the maximum density of data points, effectively tracking objects based on appearance. It's used in video surveillance and human-computer interaction due to its robustness to object shape and size changes.

Q123. Describe the difference between segmentation and classification.
Answer: Classification assigns a label to an entire image, while segmentation assigns labels to each pixel, distinguishing different regions or objects within an image. Segmentation provides more detailed understanding, especially in applications like medical imaging, where identifying boundaries is crucial. Classification is useful for broader categorization, such as detecting presence of objects.

Q124. How is deep learning used in object detection?
Answer: Deep learning-based object detection combines localization and classification to identify objects and their locations in images. Models like YOLO (You Only Look Once), SSD (Single Shot Detector), and Faster R-CNN use convolutional layers to predict bounding boxes and class labels simultaneously. These methods are efficient and accurate, enabling real-time detection in applications like security, traffic monitoring, and robotics.

Q125. What is optical flow and where is it used?
Answer: Optical flow refers to the pattern of motion of objects in a visual scene caused by relative motion between the observer and the scene. It is estimated by analyzing frame-to-frame pixel intensity changes. Used in video compression, motion detection, and autonomous navigation, optical flow helps in understanding scene dynamics and object movements.

Q126. What is the role of deep learning in modern image processing?
Answer: Deep learning plays a transformative role in modern image processing by enabling automatic feature extraction and pattern recognition from raw image data. Convolutional Neural Networks (CNNs), a deep learning architecture, are particularly effective in tasks such as object detection, image classification, and segmentation. Unlike traditional image processing methods, deep learning models learn hierarchical features directly from large datasets without manual intervention. This leads to higher accuracy and adaptability to complex real-world image data, making deep learning essential in applications like facial recognition, autonomous driving, and medical image analysis.

Q127. Explain the term "semantic segmentation" in computer vision.
Answer: Semantic segmentation is a computer vision technique that involves classifying each pixel in an image into a predefined category. Unlike traditional classification, which labels entire images, semantic

segmentation provides a detailed understanding by recognizing the boundaries and locations of objects within the image. It is widely used in applications like autonomous vehicles (for identifying road lanes, pedestrians), medical imaging (for organ or tumor detection), and satellite imagery analysis. Techniques such as Fully Convolutional Networks (FCNs) and U-Net are commonly used for semantic segmentation tasks due to their pixel-level precision.

Q128. What is the difference between semantic and instance segmentation?
Answer: Semantic segmentation assigns a class label to each pixel in an image, grouping all objects of the same class together without distinguishing between separate instances. In contrast, instance segmentation not only classifies pixels but also distinguishes between individual objects of the same category. For example, in an image with multiple dogs, semantic segmentation labels all dog pixels as "dog," whereas instance segmentation identifies each dog separately (dog 1, dog 2, etc.). Instance segmentation combines object detection with semantic segmentation and is crucial in applications that require detailed object differentiation.

Q129. How does a region proposal network (RPN) work in object detection?
Answer: A Region Proposal Network (RPN) is a component of object detection models like Faster R-CNN that generates candidate regions (also called region proposals) likely to contain objects. RPN works by sliding a small network over the convolutional feature map and predicting objectness scores and bounding box coordinates for anchors at each position. These proposals are then refined and passed to a detection network for final classification. RPN significantly speeds up the object detection process by eliminating the need for external region proposal methods and making the architecture end-to-end trainable.

Q130. What is the purpose of max pooling in Convolutional Neural Networks (CNNs)?
Answer: Max pooling is a downsampling technique used in CNNs to reduce the spatial dimensions of feature maps while retaining the most important information. It works by selecting the maximum value within a defined window (e.g., 2×2) and discarding the rest. This operation helps reduce the computational complexity, mitigates overfitting, and introduces spatial invariance, which means the model becomes more robust to small translations in the image. Max pooling layers are typically placed between convolutional layers in a CNN to progressively reduce the feature map size and enhance generalization.

Q131. What is YOLO in object detection?
Answer: YOLO (You Only Look Once) is a real-time object detection algorithm that frames object detection as a single regression problem. Unlike traditional methods that use region proposals and then classify each, YOLO processes the entire image at once and simultaneously predicts bounding boxes and class probabilities. It divides the image into a grid and predicts multiple bounding boxes and class confidences for each cell. YOLO is known for its high speed and decent accuracy, making it suitable for real-time applications such as surveillance, robotics, and autonomous vehicles.

Q132. Define the concept of receptive field in CNNs.
Answer: The receptive field in a CNN refers to the region of the input image that affects a particular output neuron in the feature map. It determines how much context the network considers when computing features at a specific layer. As the depth of the network increases, the receptive field also increases, allowing neurons to capture more complex patterns. A larger receptive field helps the network understand spatial hierarchies and dependencies within the image, which is essential for tasks like object recognition and scene understanding.

Q133. What is the significance of the Softmax function in classification?
Answer: The Softmax function is a mathematical function used in the final layer of a multi-class classification model. It converts raw logits (real-valued outputs) into a probability distribution over the

predicted classes. Each output value is squashed between 0 and 1, and all probabilities sum to 1. The class with the highest probability is chosen as the predicted label. Softmax is essential in image classification tasks where multiple mutually exclusive classes are involved, ensuring the model provides interpretable and normalized class probabilities.

Q134. What is the difference between batch normalization and dropout in deep learning?
Answer: Batch normalization and dropout are two regularization techniques used in deep learning to improve model performance and prevent overfitting. Batch normalization normalizes the input of each layer to have zero mean and unit variance, accelerating training and stabilizing learning. Dropout, on the other hand, randomly deactivates a subset of neurons during training, forcing the model to learn redundant representations. While batch normalization makes training faster and more stable, dropout enhances generalization by reducing dependency on specific neurons. Both can be used together in a deep learning architecture.

Q135. Explain the difference between computer vision and image processing.
Answer: Image processing involves performing operations on images to enhance them or extract useful information, often without understanding the content. It includes techniques like filtering, noise reduction, edge detection, and transformation. Computer vision, on the other hand, focuses on enabling machines to interpret and understand visual content as humans do. It builds upon image processing and integrates machine learning, pattern recognition, and deep learning to perform tasks like object detection, image classification, and scene understanding. Essentially, image processing is a subset of the broader field of computer vision.

Chapter 5: Most Asked Questions Part-B

Q1. What is real-time image processing and where is it used?

Answer: Real-time image processing refers to the analysis and manipulation of images at the moment they are captured or streamed, with minimal delay. It is critical in applications where immediate decision-making or response is necessary, such as autonomous vehicles, medical imaging systems (like during surgery), surveillance cameras with motion detection, augmented reality (AR), and robotics. In these cases, the processing must occur at speeds matching the input stream—typically 30 frames per second or faster. Optimized algorithms and hardware acceleration (using GPUs or FPGAs) are employed to achieve this. The goal is to make systems that can react to visual input as fast as a human would.

Q2. Explain the concept of super-resolution in image processing.

Answer: Super-resolution is a technique used in image processing to enhance the resolution of an image, producing a high-resolution (HR) image from one or multiple low-resolution (LR) inputs. The process uses algorithms to reconstruct finer details that are not visible in the original low-resolution image. Techniques include interpolation methods (bicubic, bilinear), machine learning approaches like Convolutional Neural Networks (CNNs), and Generative Adversarial Networks (GANs). Super-resolution is used in medical imaging, satellite imaging, forensic analysis, and any domain where high detail is required but only low-quality input is available.

Q3. What are the advantages of using GPU in image processing tasks?

Answer: Graphics Processing Units (GPUs) are highly parallel processors originally designed for rendering graphics but are now extensively used in image processing. They offer significant speed advantages over CPUs for data-parallel tasks, such as applying filters, transformations, and convolutions. GPUs enable faster training and inference of deep learning models used in image classification and object detection. Their ability to process multiple pixels or image sections simultaneously makes them ideal for large-scale, real-time image processing tasks, thereby improving system efficiency and reducing latency.

Q4. How does background subtraction work in video surveillance systems?

Answer: Background subtraction is a technique used to detect moving objects in videos by separating the foreground from the static background. It works by maintaining a model of the background and subtracting the current frame from this model. Any significant difference is considered part of the foreground. Adaptive background modeling, like Gaussian Mixture Models (GMM), improves accuracy by learning the background over time. This method is widely used in video surveillance, traffic monitoring, and motion detection applications for tracking people, vehicles, or objects in a scene.

Q5. What is the difference between semantic segmentation and instance segmentation?

Answer: Semantic segmentation and instance segmentation are techniques in computer vision used to classify pixels in an image. Semantic segmentation assigns a class label to each pixel, treating all objects of the same class as one (e.g., all cars are labeled "car"). Instance segmentation goes a step further by distinguishing between individual objects within the same class (e.g., car1, car2, etc.). While semantic segmentation provides a global understanding of the scene, instance segmentation is crucial for applications that require object-level analysis, such as autonomous driving and medical diagnostics.

Q6. Define and explain the role of the edge detection operator in image analysis.

Answer: Edge detection operators are algorithms used to identify points in a digital image where brightness changes sharply, indicating boundaries of objects. Common operators include the Sobel, Prewitt, Canny, and Roberts operators. They calculate gradients to detect edges by highlighting regions with strong intensity contrast. Edge detection is foundational for tasks like image segmentation, object recognition, and feature extraction, as it simplifies the image while preserving its essential structure. Effective edge detection helps in understanding the shape, size, and orientation of objects in an image.

Q7. What is the role of thresholding in image segmentation?
Answer: Thresholding is a simple yet effective technique in image segmentation used to separate objects from the background. It works by converting a grayscale image into a binary image based on a chosen threshold value. Pixels above the threshold are classified as foreground (usually white), and those below as background (black). Advanced methods like Otsu's method automatically determine the optimal threshold value by minimizing intra-class variance. Thresholding is widely used in document analysis, medical imaging, and pattern recognition where contrast is sufficient.

Q8. Explain the use of optical character recognition (OCR) in image processing.
Answer: Optical Character Recognition (OCR) is the process of converting images of typed, handwritten, or printed text into machine-encoded text. It involves several image processing steps, including binarization, noise removal, text line and character segmentation, and character recognition using pattern matching or deep learning. OCR is used in document digitization, automatic number plate recognition, banking (e.g., cheque processing), and reading text in natural scenes. Modern OCR engines like Tesseract use advanced algorithms and neural networks to achieve high accuracy.

Q9. How are image pyramids used in computer vision?
Answer: Image pyramids are multi-scale representations of an image where successive layers are smaller in size and resolution. There are two types: Gaussian pyramids (used for smoothing and reducing image size) and Laplacian pyramids (used for reconstructing and analyzing fine image details). They are used in applications like image blending, object detection (to detect objects at different scales), and image compression. By working on smaller versions of the image, algorithms can be made more efficient and robust to scale variations.

Q10. What is the purpose of morphological operations in image processing?
Answer: Morphological operations are used to process images based on their shapes and structures. Common operations include dilation, erosion, opening, and closing, which are applied to binary or grayscale images using a structuring element. These operations help in noise removal, filling gaps, extracting skeletons, and separating touching objects. Morphological transformations are widely used in applications such as medical imaging, character recognition, and object segmentation where the shape of objects is important for analysis.

Q11. What are the primary goals of image enhancement in image processing?
Answer: The primary goals of image enhancement are to improve the visual appearance of an image or to convert an image into a form better suited for analysis by a human or machine. Enhancement techniques aim to increase contrast, remove noise, sharpen features, and emphasize edges or other significant structures. These improvements are especially crucial in medical imaging, satellite imaging, and forensic science, where clearer visuals aid in more accurate diagnosis or interpretation.

Q12. How does thresholding work in segmentation techniques?
Answer: Thresholding is a segmentation technique that converts a grayscale image into a binary image based on a threshold value. Pixels with intensity values above the threshold are assigned one value (e.g., white), and those below are assigned another (e.g., black). This method is widely used for separating objects from the background and is especially useful when object and background have distinguishable intensity ranges. Adaptive thresholding and Otsu's method are common variations that enhance segmentation accuracy in varying lighting conditions.

Q13. What are the different types of color spaces used in image processing?
Answer: Different color spaces include RGB (Red, Green, Blue), HSV (Hue, Saturation, Value), CMY/CMYK (Cyan, Magenta, Yellow, Key), YCbCr, and Lab. RGB is commonly used for display devices, while HSV is preferred for color-based segmentation and detection. YCbCr is widely used in image compression and broadcasting due to its separation of luminance and chrominance. Choosing the right color space helps simplify processing and improve the accuracy of color-based image analysis.

Q14. What is the purpose of histogram equalization?
Answer: Histogram equalization is used to enhance the contrast of an image by redistributing pixel intensity values. It spreads out the most frequent intensity values, allowing areas of lower contrast to gain higher visibility. This technique is especially effective for images with backgrounds and foregrounds that are both bright or both dark. It is widely applied in medical and satellite imaging where contrast improvement is vital for detailed analysis.

Q15. What is the difference between morphological dilation and erosion?
Answer: Dilation and erosion are fundamental morphological operations. Dilation adds pixels to the boundaries of objects in an image, making them grow, while erosion removes pixels on object boundaries, causing objects to shrink. These operations are typically applied to binary images and are used for tasks like noise removal, shape refinement, and object separation. Combining dilation and erosion in various sequences (e.g., opening and closing) helps achieve more sophisticated morphological transformations.

Q16. What is the role of Fourier Transform in image processing?
Answer: The Fourier Transform decomposes an image into its sine and cosine components, representing the image in the frequency domain. It allows for analyzing the spatial frequency content, helping identify periodic patterns, and is crucial in applications like image filtering, compression, and restoration. High-frequency components represent edges and details, while low-frequency components represent smooth regions. Manipulating these components enables effective noise removal and feature enhancement.

Q17. How is edge linking performed in computer vision?
Answer: Edge linking connects edge points detected by edge detectors (like Canny or Sobel) into meaningful boundaries. Techniques include Hough Transform, contour following, and graph-based methods. Edge linking ensures that fragmented edges are connected into continuous contours representing object boundaries. Accurate edge linking is essential for object detection, shape analysis, and image segmentation in real-world applications like traffic sign recognition or biomedical image analysis.

Q18. What is the significance of the Gaussian filter in image smoothing?
Answer: The Gaussian filter is a low-pass filter that reduces image noise and detail using a Gaussian function. It preserves the general structure while smoothing out noise, making it ideal for pre-processing before edge detection or segmentation. Unlike simple averaging filters, the Gaussian filter considers pixel proximity, giving higher weights to nearer pixels, resulting in natural-looking blurred images. It is widely used in computer vision pipelines for reliable feature extraction.

Q19. What is the concept of region growing in segmentation?
Answer: Region growing is a segmentation technique that groups pixels or subregions into larger regions based on predefined criteria such as intensity similarity or texture. Starting from seed points, the algorithm includes neighboring pixels that satisfy the homogeneity condition. This method is intuitive and effective for images where objects have uniform properties but requires careful selection of seed points and stopping conditions to avoid oversegmentation.

Q20. How does the Laplacian operator help in edge detection?
Answer: The Laplacian operator detects edges by measuring the second derivative of the image. It

highlights regions of rapid intensity change, making it useful for identifying edges and boundaries. Unlike first derivative methods (e.g., Sobel), which detect edge direction, the Laplacian is direction-independent and detects points where the intensity curvature changes. It is often combined with Gaussian smoothing (Laplacian of Gaussian) to reduce sensitivity to noise.

Q21. What is the use of connected component labeling?
Answer: Connected component labeling identifies and labels connected pixel regions in binary images. It assigns a unique label to each group of connected foreground pixels, enabling further analysis like counting objects, extracting features, or separating distinct components. This technique is widely used in document analysis, medical imaging, and object tracking. Two-pass algorithms and union-find methods are common implementations for efficient labeling.

Q22. How is image sharpening achieved?
Answer: Image sharpening enhances edges and fine details by emphasizing high-frequency components. Techniques include using high-pass filters, Laplacian filters, or unsharp masking. These methods increase contrast along edges, making features more prominent. Sharpening is essential in applications where detail visibility is critical, such as satellite imagery and medical diagnostics. However, excessive sharpening may introduce artifacts or noise, so balance is necessary.

Q23. What is the purpose of image compression?
Answer: Image compression reduces the file size of images to save storage and bandwidth while maintaining acceptable quality. It is achieved through lossy (e.g., JPEG) and lossless (e.g., PNG) methods. Lossy compression removes perceptually insignificant data, while lossless retains all information. Compression is crucial in web applications, mobile devices, and cloud storage. Effective compression balances image fidelity with reduced resource usage.

Q24. What are Gabor filters and where are they used?
Answer: Gabor filters are linear filters used for texture analysis, edge detection, and feature extraction. They capture both spatial and frequency information, making them useful in analyzing image texture and orientation. Gabor filters are applied in face recognition, fingerprint analysis, and iris recognition due to their ability to mimic human visual perception. Their multi-resolution and multi-orientation characteristics allow for robust feature representation.

Q25. What are the differences between optical flow and motion estimation?
Answer: Optical flow estimates the motion of each pixel between frames based on brightness patterns, whereas motion estimation generally finds the global or block-wise movement of objects. Optical flow provides dense, pixel-level motion fields and is useful in autonomous driving and video stabilization. Motion estimation, used in video compression, is more approximate and computationally efficient. Both methods are key in video analysis and surveillance.

Q26. What is meant by corner detection in computer vision?
Answer: Corner detection identifies points in an image where the intensity changes in multiple directions, usually indicating object corners or interest points. Techniques like Harris corner detector and Shi-Tomasi algorithm are commonly used. Corners are essential for tracking, object recognition, and stitching images. Their stability and distinctiveness make them ideal for feature matching across frames or different images.

Q27. Explain the difference between global and local thresholding.
Answer: Global thresholding uses a single threshold value for the entire image, while local thresholding calculates thresholds for small regions, making it more effective under uneven lighting. Global thresholding is simple and fast but may fail when background illumination varies. Local methods like adaptive thresholding address these limitations and provide better segmentation results in complex images.

Q28. What is the function of the Hough Transform?
Answer: The Hough Transform is used to detect geometric shapes like lines, circles, or ellipses in an image. It maps points in the image space to curves in the parameter space and finds the most likely shape parameters based on accumulations. Widely used in industrial inspection, autonomous driving, and lane detection, Hough Transform is robust against noise and partial occlusion.

Q29. What is image registration?
Answer: Image registration aligns two or more images of the same scene taken at different times, viewpoints, or sensors. It involves geometric transformation and interpolation to match corresponding features or intensity patterns. Registration is vital in medical imaging (e.g., MRI and CT fusion), remote sensing, and computer vision tasks like panorama creation. Accurate registration ensures meaningful comparison and analysis.

Q30. How does the mean shift algorithm work in segmentation?
Answer: The mean shift algorithm is a non-parametric clustering technique that iteratively shifts data points toward the mode (highest density) in a feature space. In image segmentation, it groups pixels with similar features like color and spatial proximity. Mean shift does not require prior knowledge of the number of clusters and adapts well to arbitrary shapes, making it effective for object tracking and color segmentation.

Q41. What is the role of keypoint detection in image matching?
Answer: Keypoint detection is critical in image matching as it identifies distinct and stable points in an image that can be reliably recognized across different views, scales, or lighting conditions. These keypoints serve as anchors for comparing and aligning images. Algorithms like SIFT, SURF, and ORB detect keypoints and compute descriptors for matching them across images. This process enables applications such as panorama stitching, object recognition, and 3D reconstruction by ensuring accurate and consistent feature correspondence between image pairs.

Q42. What is the use of the ORB algorithm in computer vision?
Answer: ORB (Oriented FAST and Rotated BRIEF) is an efficient and rotation-invariant keypoint detector and descriptor used in computer vision tasks. It combines the FAST keypoint detector with the BRIEF descriptor and introduces orientation compensation for robustness. ORB is especially favored for its speed and computational efficiency, making it suitable for real-time applications such as visual SLAM (Simultaneous Localization and Mapping), object tracking, and mobile augmented reality systems. It is often used as a free and fast alternative to SIFT and SURF.

Q43. What is the purpose of the RANSAC algorithm in image processing?
Answer: RANSAC (Random Sample Consensus) is an iterative algorithm used to estimate parameters of a mathematical model from a set of observed data that may contain outliers. In image processing and computer vision, RANSAC is frequently used in applications such as estimating homographies, fitting fundamental matrices, or aligning feature points during image stitching. Its strength lies in its robustness against noise and its ability to ignore outliers while selecting the best model fitting the majority of data points.

Q44. How is camera calibration performed in computer vision?
Answer: Camera calibration is the process of estimating the intrinsic and extrinsic parameters of a camera to map 3D world coordinates to 2D image coordinates accurately. This involves capturing multiple images of a known calibration pattern (like a checkerboard), detecting key features, and using algorithms such as Zhang's method to compute parameters like focal length, optical center, lens distortion coefficients, and rotation and translation vectors. Calibration is essential for 3D reconstruction, augmented reality, and accurate measurements in vision systems.

Q45. What is the significance of optical flow in video analysis?
Answer: Optical flow refers to the pattern of apparent motion of objects, surfaces, or edges in a video sequence, caused by the relative motion between the camera and the scene. It is used to analyze and estimate motion between consecutive frames. Applications include object tracking, motion detection, video compression, and activity recognition. Techniques such as Lucas-Kanade and Horn-Schunck algorithms help compute optical flow fields to capture movement patterns over time, enabling dynamic scene understanding.

Q46. What are stereo vision systems, and how do they work?
Answer: Stereo vision systems use two or more cameras to capture images from different viewpoints, mimicking human binocular vision to perceive depth. By identifying corresponding points between images and computing disparities, stereo systems estimate the depth of objects in the scene. This technique is used in robotics, autonomous vehicles, and 3D reconstruction to understand the spatial arrangement of environments. Accurate calibration, rectification, and disparity map generation are key components of a stereo vision pipeline.

Q47. What is image pyramiding, and why is it important?
Answer: Image pyramiding is a technique in image processing where an image is represented at multiple resolutions in a hierarchical structure, typically in Gaussian and Laplacian forms. Each level of the pyramid contains a progressively reduced resolution version of the image. It is crucial for multi-scale image analysis, efficient feature detection, image blending, and object tracking. Image pyramids allow algorithms to process different levels of detail, enhancing performance and robustness in tasks like image registration and compression.

Q48. What are active contours (snakes) in computer vision?
Answer: Active contours, or snakes, are curves that move within images to find object boundaries based on energy minimization. These curves are initialized near the target object and iteratively adjusted by internal forces (ensuring smoothness) and external forces (derived from image gradients or features). Active contours are used in image segmentation to accurately delineate object shapes, particularly in medical imaging and object tracking, due to their ability to conform to complex and irregular boundaries.

Q49. What are the advantages of using neural networks in image processing?
Answer: Neural networks, particularly convolutional neural networks (CNNs), offer numerous advantages in image processing tasks. They automatically learn hierarchical features from raw pixel data, eliminating the need for manual feature engineering. CNNs excel in tasks like image classification, segmentation, object detection, and style transfer. Their ability to generalize from large datasets makes them powerful tools for robust image analysis. Moreover, deep architectures such as ResNet or UNet further enhance performance in complex visual recognition problems.

Q50. How is 3D reconstruction achieved from 2D images?
Answer: 3D reconstruction from 2D images involves estimating the three-dimensional structure of a scene using one or more 2D images. Techniques include stereo vision, structure from motion (SfM), and photometric stereo. These methods rely on extracting and matching keypoints across multiple views, estimating camera positions, and triangulating points in 3D space. The result is a dense or sparse point cloud, which can be further processed into 3D meshes or models. Applications include archaeology, virtual reality, robotics, and animation.

Q51. What is the concept of image stitching in computer vision?
Answer: Image stitching is the process of combining multiple images with overlapping fields of view to produce a single panoramic or high-resolution image. It involves steps like image registration, warping,

blending, and exposure compensation. Feature detection algorithms (like SIFT or ORB) are used to find keypoints and match them across images. The matched features help align images geometrically. This technique is widely used in panoramic photography, 360-degree imaging, satellite image processing, and virtual tours.

Q52. What is motion segmentation in video analysis?
Answer: Motion segmentation is the process of separating moving objects from the background in a video sequence. It helps in identifying regions that undergo motion and is critical for tasks like object tracking, surveillance, and gesture recognition. Techniques include background subtraction, optical flow, and frame differencing. More advanced methods involve using deep learning models to detect and classify motion patterns. Accurate segmentation allows better understanding of dynamic scenes in real time.

Q53. What is meant by disparity map in stereo vision?
Answer: A disparity map is an image that represents the difference in pixel positions of the same object in the left and right images of a stereo vision system. The disparity value at each pixel is inversely proportional to the depth of the scene point it represents. Computing the disparity map is a crucial step in depth estimation and 3D reconstruction. High disparity means the object is closer, and low disparity indicates it is farther from the cameras.

Q54. How is homography used in image processing?
Answer: Homography refers to a transformation that maps points from one image plane to another, assuming both images view the same planar surface from different perspectives. It is represented by a 3x3 matrix and is used in tasks like image stitching, perspective correction, and object tracking. Homography is estimated using matched keypoints between two images, typically with the help of RANSAC to remove outliers. It is essential for aligning images in mosaicing and AR applications.

Q55. What is the role of edge orientation histograms in image descriptors?
Answer: Edge orientation histograms, such as those used in the Histogram of Oriented Gradients (HOG) descriptor, capture the distribution of gradient directions in an image region. They are used to characterize the local shape and appearance of objects by summarizing edge information. This technique is particularly effective in human detection, object recognition, and image classification. It provides robustness to small variations in pose and lighting by focusing on the structural layout of edges.

Q56. What is the use of the Kalman filter in object tracking?
Answer: The Kalman filter is an optimal recursive data processing algorithm used in object tracking to estimate the position and velocity of a moving object over time. It predicts the future state of the object and corrects the estimate using new measurements. The filter assumes Gaussian noise and works efficiently in linear dynamic systems. In computer vision, it is widely used in real-time tracking applications, such as surveillance, robotics, and autonomous vehicles, due to its low computational cost.

Q57. What is the significance of image thresholding in segmentation?
Answer: Image thresholding is a simple yet effective technique used in segmentation to convert grayscale images into binary images. By choosing a threshold value, pixels are classified as foreground or background depending on whether their intensity is above or below the threshold. Techniques include global thresholding, adaptive thresholding, and Otsu's method. It is useful for isolating objects of interest in applications such as OCR (Optical Character Recognition), medical imaging, and document analysis.

Q58. What is the function of image dilation in morphological processing?
Answer: Image dilation is a morphological operation that grows or thickens objects in a binary image. It works by placing a structuring element over each pixel and setting the output pixel to the maximum value of the neighborhood. Dilation is used to close small holes, connect broken parts, and emphasize features in

an image. It is often used in conjunction with erosion in tasks such as edge detection, noise removal, and object extraction.

Q59. What is the difference between supervised and unsupervised segmentation?
Answer: Supervised segmentation uses labeled data and machine learning models to segment images based on learned patterns. It requires prior training and performs well when data is consistent. Unsupervised segmentation, on the other hand, does not use labeled data and relies on algorithms like K-means clustering, mean shift, or region growing to group pixels based on similarity in color, texture, or intensity. Unsupervised methods are flexible and adaptable but may be less accurate than supervised approaches.

Q60. What is camera pose estimation in computer vision?
Answer: Camera pose estimation refers to determining the position and orientation of a camera relative to a known world coordinate system or a 3D scene. It is essential for augmented reality, robotics, and 3D reconstruction. Pose estimation uses 2D-3D correspondences between image points and world points, solved using algorithms like PnP (Perspective-n-Point). Accurate pose estimation enables virtual objects to be correctly overlaid in AR applications and allows robots to navigate and interact with their environment.

Q71. What is the role of contour detection in computer vision?
Answer: Contour detection involves identifying the boundaries of objects in an image. It provides important shape information and helps in object recognition, tracking, and segmentation. Techniques like OpenCV's findContours() use edge-detected images to extract the outlines. Contours can be analyzed to determine geometric features such as area, perimeter, centroid, and orientation. This is especially useful in medical imaging, pattern recognition, and gesture analysis, where accurate object boundaries are essential.

Q72. What is vanishing point detection in image analysis?
Answer: Vanishing point detection refers to identifying the point in an image where parallel lines appear to converge due to perspective. It is crucial in understanding scene geometry, depth estimation, and camera calibration. Vanishing points help determine the orientation of objects and are used in 3D reconstruction, road detection in autonomous driving, and architectural analysis. Line detection techniques like the Hough Transform are commonly used to find vanishing points.

Q73. How are Gaussian Mixture Models used in background subtraction?
Answer: Gaussian Mixture Models (GMM) model the distribution of pixel intensities over time to distinguish background from foreground in video sequences. Each pixel is modeled as a mixture of Gaussians, allowing for dynamic background changes like lighting or moving leaves. Foreground is detected when a pixel does not match any of the background distributions. GMMs provide robust background modeling in surveillance, traffic monitoring, and motion analysis.

Q74. What is the significance of feature scaling in computer vision models?
Answer: Feature scaling ensures that input features contribute equally to the learning process, especially in machine learning models used for image classification or object detection. In image processing, pixel values or extracted features like SIFT, HOG, or LBP may have different scales. Normalizing them improves convergence and model performance. Techniques like min-max normalization and standardization are commonly used to bring features into a similar scale before training.

Q75. What are the applications of saliency detection?
Answer: Saliency detection identifies the most attention-grabbing regions in an image or video. It mimics human visual attention and is used in image compression, object recognition, visual tracking, and adaptive image display. Salient regions are often used as a cue to focus computational resources on important areas. Techniques include spectral residual methods, frequency domain analysis, and deep learning-based models trained to detect salient objects.

Q76. How is the integral image used in fast computation?
Answer: The integral image, or summed-area table, is a data structure that allows rapid computation of the sum of values in a rectangular subset of a grid. It's particularly useful in real-time object detection, like the Viola-Jones face detection framework. Once the integral image is computed, the sum of any sub-region can be obtained in constant time, enabling efficient feature calculation over image patches.

Q77. What is the role of active contour models (snakes)?
Answer: Active contour models, or snakes, are used for delineating object boundaries in images by evolving a curve toward the object edge based on energy minimization. Internal energy enforces smoothness, while external energy attracts the curve to edges or gradients. Snakes are useful in medical imaging, object segmentation, and shape modeling, especially when precise boundary extraction is needed in noisy or low-contrast images.

Q78. What is the concept of image moments in object analysis?
Answer: Image moments are scalar quantities that provide information about the shape, orientation, and area of an object in an image. Moments like spatial moments, central moments, and Hu moments are used for object recognition, shape matching, and centroid calculation. These descriptors are invariant to transformations like rotation, scale, and translation, making them useful in pattern recognition and image classification tasks.

Q79. What is the difference between keypoint detection and keypoint matching?
Answer: Keypoint detection identifies distinctive points in an image that are stable under transformations, such as corners or blobs. Keypoint matching involves comparing these keypoints across different images to find correspondences. Detection uses algorithms like SIFT, SURF, or ORB, while matching is done using metrics like Euclidean distance or Hamming distance. This process is critical in tasks such as image stitching, object tracking, and stereo vision.

Q80. What is a confusion matrix and how is it used in evaluating vision models?
Answer: A confusion matrix is a performance evaluation tool for classification models, showing the counts of true positives, true negatives, false positives, and false negatives. In computer vision, it helps analyze model accuracy, precision, recall, and F1-score for image classification tasks. It provides insights into which classes are being confused, helping improve training data or model architecture for better performance.

Q81. What is the use of semantic segmentation in computer vision?
Answer: Semantic segmentation involves labeling each pixel of an image with a class label, providing detailed understanding of scene components. It is used in autonomous driving (e.g., identifying roads, cars, pedestrians), medical imaging (organ or tumor segmentation), and AR applications. Unlike object detection, which uses bounding boxes, semantic segmentation offers pixel-level precision, achieved using deep learning models like FCN, U-Net, or DeepLab.

Q82. What is the function of adaptive histogram equalization?
Answer: Adaptive histogram equalization improves contrast in images by enhancing local contrast in small regions rather than the entire image. It works well for images with varying illumination or poor lighting conditions. A popular variant, CLAHE (Contrast Limited Adaptive Histogram Equalization), prevents over-amplification of noise. It is useful in medical imaging, satellite image enhancement, and preprocessing tasks in computer vision pipelines.

Q83. What is the purpose of color space conversion in image processing?
Answer: Color space conversion transforms image data from one representation to another (e.g., RGB to

HSV, YCbCr, Lab). Different color spaces are better suited for specific tasks. HSV separates color from intensity, helpful in object detection under varying lighting. YCbCr is used in compression (JPEG), and Lab provides perceptual uniformity. Converting color space aids in segmentation, filtering, and feature extraction.

Q84. What are the common challenges in video surveillance systems using computer vision?
Answer: Challenges in video surveillance include poor lighting, occlusion, motion blur, and varying weather conditions. Real-time processing of large data volumes requires efficient algorithms. Background modeling must adapt to changes, and multiple object tracking needs robust re-identification. Ensuring privacy and handling low-resolution video are also concerns. Deep learning and edge computing are helping to overcome many of these limitations.

Q85. What is the use of optical character recognition (OCR)?
Answer: OCR is a technique that extracts text from images or scanned documents using pattern recognition and machine learning. It converts printed or handwritten text into machine-readable format. OCR is used in document digitization, license plate recognition, and assistive technology for the visually impaired. Advanced OCR systems use deep learning for improved accuracy on complex layouts and diverse fonts.

Q86. What is the function of Hough Transform in image processing?
Answer: Hough Transform is a feature extraction technique used to detect simple shapes like lines, circles, or ellipses in images. It transforms edge points into parameter space and accumulates votes for possible shapes. The most voted parameters correspond to detected shapes. It's widely used in lane detection, coin recognition, and industrial inspection. Probabilistic and Generalized Hough variants extend its utility to more complex cases.

Q87. How is RANSAC used in image processing?
Answer: RANSAC (Random Sample Consensus) is an iterative algorithm used to estimate parameters of a mathematical model in the presence of outliers. In image processing, it is commonly used in robust homography estimation, fundamental matrix computation, and feature matching. RANSAC selects random subsets of data, fits a model, and evaluates its consensus. It improves accuracy by excluding noise and mismatched data points.

Q88. What is object detection and how is it implemented?
Answer: Object detection identifies and localizes objects within an image using bounding boxes and class labels. It is implemented using deep learning models like YOLO (You Only Look Once), SSD (Single Shot Detector), and Faster R-CNN. These models combine classification and regression tasks, enabling real-time or high-accuracy detection. Applications include face detection, vehicle tracking, and retail analytics.

Q89. What is template matching in computer vision?
Answer: Template matching is a technique for finding regions in an image that match a given template or pattern. It slides the template over the image and compares each patch using similarity measures like cross-correlation or sum of squared differences. While simple, it's sensitive to scale, rotation, and illumination changes. It's used in character recognition, quality control, and object tracking.

Q90. What is the role of deep learning in image processing?
Answer: Deep learning has revolutionized image processing by enabling end-to-end learning of features and decision-making. Convolutional Neural Networks (CNNs) are particularly suited for tasks like classification, detection, and segmentation. Pretrained models like VGG, ResNet, and EfficientNet offer state-of-the-art accuracy. Deep learning excels in complex scenarios with large datasets, automating feature extraction and delivering superior performance over traditional methods.

Q91. What is morphological gradient in image processing?
Answer: Morphological gradient is the difference between the dilation and erosion of an image. It highlights the edges of objects by computing the boundary pixels. Mathematically, it is expressed as:
Gradient = Dilation(image) - Erosion(image)
This technique is useful in edge detection, object segmentation, and shape analysis. It helps extract clear boundaries of features in binary or grayscale images and is especially used in preprocessing tasks before applying recognition algorithms.

Q92. What is the difference between semantic and instance segmentation?
Answer: Semantic segmentation labels every pixel in an image according to a class (e.g., all "cars" as one label), whereas instance segmentation not only classifies but also differentiates between separate instances of the same class (e.g., car1, car2). Semantic segmentation is useful for general scene understanding, while instance segmentation is crucial when individual object tracking or counting is needed, such as in autonomous vehicles or crowd analysis.

Q93. What is edge linking and how is it performed?
Answer: Edge linking connects broken or fragmented edges in an image to form continuous boundaries. After edge detection (like using Canny), pixels are grouped based on continuity, gradient direction, and proximity. Techniques include thresholding, Hough Transform, and graph-based methods. Edge linking improves contour detection and is important for object recognition, shape extraction, and boundary-based segmentation tasks.

Q94. What are motion vectors in video processing?
Answer: Motion vectors represent the movement of objects between frames in a video. They are essential in motion estimation, video compression (like in MPEG, H.264), and object tracking. By analyzing blocks of pixels, motion vectors estimate how a block has moved between frames. This allows for efficient video encoding and supports motion-based analysis such as activity recognition or surveillance.

Q95. What is the difference between affine and projective transformation?
Answer: Affine transformation preserves parallelism and includes rotation, translation, scaling, and shearing. Projective transformation, on the other hand, includes perspective effects and can map lines to points or change the convergence of lines (like vanishing points). Affine is simpler and widely used in image registration, while projective is more general and suitable for perspective correction and 3D projection in vision tasks.

Q96. How is face recognition different from face detection?
Answer: Face detection involves locating the position of faces in an image or video (e.g., drawing bounding boxes), while face recognition goes further to identify or verify the identity of the person. Detection uses methods like Haar cascades or deep CNNs, whereas recognition often uses embeddings (e.g., via FaceNet) and compares them using classifiers or distance measures. Recognition is used in authentication, surveillance, and tagging applications.

Q97. What are image descriptors in computer vision?
Answer: Image descriptors are numerical representations of image features that summarize key information such as texture, shape, or color. They enable comparison between images and are used in tasks like classification, retrieval, and matching. Examples include SIFT, HOG, SURF, and LBP. Descriptors play a critical role in building robust models that can generalize well across varying image conditions.

Q98. What is the significance of the Laplacian of Gaussian operator?
Answer: The Laplacian of Gaussian (LoG) operator is used to detect edges by combining Gaussian smoothing with the Laplacian edge detector. First, it reduces noise using a Gaussian filter, then applies the

Laplacian to highlight areas of rapid intensity change. This operator is especially good for detecting blobs and fine edges, making it useful in medical imaging and biological shape detection.

Q99. How are recurrent neural networks (RNNs) used in computer vision?
Answer: Although primarily used for sequence data, RNNs are applied in computer vision for tasks involving temporal dynamics like video analysis, action recognition, and image captioning. RNNs (especially LSTM and GRU variants) can model dependencies across frames in video or generate sequential descriptions for images. In combination with CNNs, RNNs allow for comprehensive spatial-temporal modeling.

Q100. What is the difference between supervised and unsupervised learning in vision?
Answer: In supervised learning, the model is trained using labeled images (e.g., "dog", "car"), allowing it to learn direct mappings from input to output. It's used in classification, detection, and segmentation. Unsupervised learning, however, works without labeled data and identifies patterns or clusters (e.g., grouping similar textures or shapes). It's useful in anomaly detection, feature learning, and image clustering where labeled data is scarce.

Q101. What is the use of GANs in image generation?
Answer: Generative Adversarial Networks (GANs) are used to generate realistic synthetic images by training two neural networks: a generator and a discriminator. The generator creates fake images, while the discriminator evaluates their authenticity. Over time, the generator learns to produce images indistinguishable from real ones. GANs are used in applications like image-to-image translation, super-resolution, style transfer, and creating realistic human faces or artwork.

Q102. How does depth estimation work in stereo vision?
Answer: In stereo vision, depth estimation involves comparing two images captured from slightly different viewpoints (like human eyes) to compute the disparity between corresponding pixels. The disparity is inversely proportional to the depth of objects. Techniques like block matching, semi-global matching, or deep learning-based disparity estimation are used. Depth maps created help in 3D reconstruction, autonomous navigation, and augmented reality.

Q103. What is an epipolar line in stereo imaging?
Answer: An epipolar line is a line on one image where the corresponding point from another image (in a stereo pair) must lie, based on the camera geometry. This reduces the 2D search for correspondence to a 1D problem along the line. Epipolar geometry is fundamental in stereo matching, 3D reconstruction, and camera calibration tasks in computer vision.

Q104. How is image alignment achieved in mosaicking?
Answer: Image alignment in mosaicking involves matching overlapping parts of multiple images to create a seamless panoramic view. This is done using keypoint detection (like SIFT or ORB), feature matching, estimation of homography matrix, and image warping. Once aligned, images are blended using techniques like multi-band blending. Mosaicking is used in panoramic photography, remote sensing, and medical imaging.

Q105. What is image deblurring and how is it performed?
Answer: Image deblurring aims to restore sharp images from blurred ones caused by motion, defocus, or camera shake. Techniques include inverse filtering, Wiener filtering, blind deconvolution, and deep learning models like DeblurGAN. Accurate estimation of the blur kernel is crucial. Deblurring is used in forensic analysis, surveillance footage enhancement, and improving photo quality.

Q106. What is the function of a lookup table (LUT) in image processing?
Answer: A lookup table (LUT) is used to map input pixel values to new output values for tasks like contrast enhancement, color correction, or thresholding. LUTs enable fast and efficient transformation by precomputing the desired output for each input intensity. They are commonly used in grayscale adjustments, thermal imaging, and image post-processing workflows.

Q107. How is object tracking different from detection?
Answer: Object detection identifies and locates objects in individual frames, whereas object tracking maintains the identity and position of objects across multiple frames. Tracking involves initializing with detected objects and updating their positions using algorithms like Kalman filter, Mean-Shift, or deep trackers (e.g., SORT, DeepSORT). It is vital in video surveillance, traffic monitoring, and activity recognition.

Q108. What is meant by multi-scale image representation?
Answer: Multi-scale representation involves analyzing an image at different resolutions or scales to capture both fine and coarse details. Gaussian pyramid and Laplacian pyramid are common techniques. It is beneficial in feature detection, object recognition, and image compression, allowing algorithms to process images efficiently and robustly under scale changes.

Q109. What is the concept of attention in vision transformers?
Answer: In Vision Transformers (ViT), attention mechanisms allow the model to focus on specific regions of the image by computing weighted importance of different patches. Self-attention captures long-range dependencies and context within the image. This approach has achieved state-of-the-art performance in classification, segmentation, and detection by learning relationships between spatial regions more effectively than CNNs.

Q110. How are optical illusions studied in computer vision?
Answer: Optical illusions provide insights into human perception and are used to test and develop vision models. By analyzing how humans misinterpret visual stimuli, researchers design algorithms that mimic human vision or detect perceptual errors. Understanding illusions helps improve models in depth perception, shape understanding, and scene interpretation.

Q111. What is saliency detection and its purpose?
Answer: Saliency detection identifies the most visually significant or attention-grabbing regions in an image. It mimics human visual attention and is used in object detection, video compression, and image cropping. Methods include contrast-based models, frequency-tuned saliency, and deep learning approaches. Salient regions help reduce computational load by focusing only on important parts.

Q112. What are descriptors like LBP and their uses?
Answer: Local Binary Patterns (LBP) is a texture descriptor that compares each pixel with its neighbors and encodes it into a binary pattern. It is robust to illumination changes and widely used in face recognition, texture classification, and defect detection. Descriptors like LBP capture local texture features and are effective in low-complexity applications.

Q113. What is the purpose of region growing in segmentation?
Answer: Region growing is a segmentation technique that groups neighboring pixels based on similarity in intensity, color, or texture. It starts with a seed point and expands as long as neighboring pixels meet similarity criteria. This method is used in medical imaging (e.g., tumor boundary detection) and remote sensing for separating homogeneous areas.

Q114. How is background subtraction used in video processing?
Answer: Background subtraction identifies moving objects by comparing each frame to a background model. Differences indicate foreground objects. Techniques include frame differencing, Gaussian Mixture Models, and deep learning-based segmentation. It's essential in surveillance, traffic monitoring, and gesture recognition, allowing efficient tracking and activity detection.

Q115. What is the significance of keypoint matching?
Answer: Keypoint matching finds correspondences between images based on local features like corners or blobs. Techniques like SIFT, SURF, and ORB are used for detecting and describing keypoints. Matched points help in image stitching, 3D reconstruction, and object recognition. It enables alignment and comparison of scenes from different viewpoints.

Q116. What is camera calibration and why is it necessary?
Answer: Camera calibration determines the intrinsic and extrinsic parameters of a camera, such as focal length, lens distortion, and position. Accurate calibration allows mapping 3D world points to 2D image coordinates. It is essential for 3D reconstruction, AR, robotics, and stereo vision. Calibration ensures spatial accuracy in visual measurements.

Q117. How is segmentation used in self-driving cars?
Answer: In autonomous vehicles, segmentation identifies road lanes, vehicles, pedestrians, and traffic signs by classifying each pixel. Semantic and instance segmentation help understand the environment, enabling path planning and obstacle avoidance. Deep learning models like Mask R-CNN or DeepLab are widely used for accurate scene interpretation in real-time.

Q118. What are the challenges in 3D reconstruction from images?
Answer: 3D reconstruction from images faces challenges like occlusion, varying lighting, lack of texture, and camera calibration errors. Accurate depth estimation, feature matching, and model fitting are crucial. Techniques like Structure from Motion (SfM), Multi-View Stereo (MVS), and neural rendering help overcome these challenges for applications in AR, VR, and digital modeling.

Q119. What is the importance of motion segmentation?
Answer: Motion segmentation separates moving objects from the background in a video. It is used in activity recognition, video surveillance, and scene understanding. Optical flow, background subtraction, and clustering of motion vectors are common methods. Motion segmentation helps isolate dynamic elements for further analysis or tracking.

Q120. How are adversarial examples used in image processing research?
Answer: Adversarial examples are images modified with small perturbations that cause machine learning models to misclassify them. They expose vulnerabilities in models and are used to study model robustness and develop defenses. Understanding adversarial attacks is vital for building secure vision systems in critical areas like healthcare and autonomous driving.

Q121. What is photometric stereo and its application?
Answer: Photometric stereo estimates the surface normals of an object using multiple images captured under different lighting conditions. It helps reconstruct 3D surface geometry without needing multiple viewpoints. Applications include facial modeling, archaeological artifact reconstruction, and industrial surface inspection.

Q122. How is image retrieval performed in large datasets?
Answer: Image retrieval involves finding visually similar images from a database given a query image. Feature extraction (like color histograms, deep features) and similarity measures (Euclidean distance,

cosine similarity) are used. Advanced systems use hashing and indexing for faster search. Image retrieval is used in e-commerce, copyright detection, and digital libraries.

Q123. What is image warping and where is it used?
Answer: Image warping alters the spatial arrangement of pixels to change the shape or alignment of an image. It uses transformation matrices to map source to destination coordinates. Warping is used in panoramic stitching, perspective correction, augmented reality, and morphing effects in media.

Q124. What are the limitations of CNNs in vision tasks?
Answer: CNNs, though powerful, have limitations such as sensitivity to adversarial attacks, requirement for large labeled datasets, lack of spatial hierarchy understanding, and difficulty capturing global context. They struggle with reasoning and 3D understanding compared to vision transformers. Research is ongoing to improve generalization and robustness.

Q125. What is the future of computer vision and its impact on society?
Answer: The future of computer vision includes advancements in real-time 3D perception, human-computer interaction, and integration with AI for decision-making. It will impact healthcare (automated diagnostics), transportation (autonomous vehicles), security (biometric recognition), and agriculture (yield prediction). Ethical considerations and privacy concerns will be critical as vision systems become more pervasive.

Printed at Repro India Ltd.